CHANG YOUR LIFE IN

C000002059

5

To my daughter Amelie, I feel privileged to be chaperoning you through this first part of your journey. May you always live a life of true choice. Love ooo!

This edition published in 2020 by
Eddison Books Limited
www.eddisonbooks.com

Text copyright © Sue Belton 2020
Design copyright © Eddison Books Limited 2020
Cover design by Georgie Hewitt

British Library Cataloguing-in-Publication data available on request.

ISBN 978-1-85906-460-3

1 3 5 7 9 10 8 6 4 2

Printed in Europe

CHANGE YOUR LIFE IN 5

PRACTICAL STEPS TO MAKING
MEANINGFUL CHANGES IN YOUR LIFE

Eddison Books Ltd

CONTENTS

FOREWORD

I began college doing an English Education major and then got totally enamoured with the theatre. Following this, I became really excited about coaching and somehow I ended up as the co-founder of a global coaching organization.

As I look back over my career, I see that it was impossible to know where I was headed. The two important things that guided me through all the crazy twists and turns of my personal yellow brick road was the determination to follow my heart and the power to choose the path that was most compelling.

Don't get me wrong, I managed to generate plenty of catastrophes and breakdowns along the way and everything was definitely not rosy all the time. Yet the ability to recover and the power to choose always steered me back on course. Now, looking back, I can see that every single brick in that road mattered and contributed mightily to a life of love, fulfillment and joy.

One of the things I like about Sue is that she has followed a similarly diverse, challenging and painful pathway. Then from the depth of her own experience, she wrote *Change Your Life in 5* because she wants people to know that they have the power to change things and to choose the life that they want.

We live in a complex time, full of uncertainty, volatility, chaos and ambiguity. It's pretty easy to get overwhelmed and feel like the only thing to do is to crawl back into bed and pull the covers over our heads. We very much need models and tools that ground and fortify us and that empower us to approach ourselves and our world with positivity and hope.

Change Your Life in 5 is such a book. Read it and more importantly, *use* it.

We all yearn for lives of richness, satisfaction and fulfillment. In *Change Your Life in 5*, Sue provides a simple, easy-to-use guide for creating precisely that. So get started right now. Be bold and begin the journey *now* to create the life you want. There is no other moment to wait for.

One of my most fervent desires is that those who CTI has touched will use what they have learned to 'pay it forward' and contribute to making the world a better place for others. That's one of the reasons I am so delighted to be writing this foreword. It gives me the chance to celebrate Sue's beautiful book as she 'pays it forward' to you.

Working with this book will generate internal harmony and fulfillment for you which will then be reflected eternally. So, as you change your life in five, you will also be making our world a little brighter and a littler more whole. In many ways, large and small, you will be 'paying it forward'. Isn't that what we all want, ultimately?

With respect and gratitude,
Karen Kimsey-House

INTRODUCTION

Choice – an act of choosing, the right or ability to choose.
Change – make or become different, exchange one thing for another.

Whatever your situation, whatever life throws at you, you always have a choice and you can *always* change it. I know this is a radical statement, but this is what I have learned from my own personal journey, and as a coach I have helped hundreds of clients do the same. When I was at my lowest, when I felt stuck and trapped and was unable to see a way out, I was lucky enough to find coaching. I discovered there is always a way out, and there is always a different, better way to live.

My story

I had been signed off work with depression and anxiety and had been put on medication. My daughter Amelie was just over a year old and my planned return to work after a year's maternity leave had gone disastrously wrong. It started with

my mum breaking her wrist: she was due to look after Amelie three days a week while I returned to work part time as a producer at the BBC. It was a job that I loved and, until I gave birth, I had spent my entire adult life studying and working very hard. I was your classic 'over-achiever' – working long hours often at the expense of my health, wellbeing and relationships.

My mother's broken wrist meant that my partner's mother had to look after Amelie while I went back to work. At the end of a long day at work, I walked into the living room to see Amelie red, flushed and floppy, sitting on the knee of a woman that wasn't me. I remember holding onto the door frame, feeling desperate for something to steady me. I couldn't leave her like that again.

I went to work the following day and the next, but I became more and more desperate,

and found it increasingly difficult to see a way out. I went to see my GP hoping for a solution. She asked me a series of questions; it was clear I was suffering from a mixture of anxiety and depression, and I was prescribed medication. I can't remember much about what followed, but I know I left my job and didn't go back.

What I do remember about that time was the feeling of sheer panic and fear. I had spent my whole life achieving, doing what many saw as a pretty impressive, glamorous job. What no one had told me was that my job would not allow me to bring up my daughter in the way I wanted. I wanted to do something meaningful and stimulating, but I also wanted to see her grow up. On a practical level, I needed to pay my part of a fairly hefty mortgage, plus bills, and I didn't know how I was going to do all of that. This situation and my mental state took its toll on my relationship with Amelie's father. Up until this point, I had always been the strong one, but now I was a mess – at home with a baby, unable even to go on public transport. I started to have panic attacks and to drink heavily. I didn't have a clue about what I was going to do. I could only manage what was necessary to get through the day and take care of my daughter.

While I was signed off, the BBC announced a round of redundancies. I knew I had to take my chance while I could. I didn't know what on Earth I would do after leaving, I just knew I had to take the opportunity to find a way out. It was both one of the easiest and one of the hardest things I've ever done. Making the decision felt like a no-brainer but afterwards the reality kicked in. I struggled with my whole

I believe we always have a choice, and can always change things, even when we think we can't.

identity: I was no longer a *producer*, but who was I? How could I lead the life I really wanted?

It was during this time that I had a chance meeting with a former colleague. She had retrained as a Life Coach and told me how much she loved it – being naturally curious about people (snap), wanting to help them (snap), and having the freedom and flexibility to work around caring for her daughter (looking good so far). It all sounded great, apart from the fact that I'd never previously been brave enough even to work freelance and forego a regular salary, let alone consider running my own coaching practice.

I had nothing else lined up, no other ideas and options on the horizon, so I decided to look into it. After a lot of digging, research and phone calls, I found the Co-Active Training Institute (CTI). I was offered a coaching session over the phone to see what it was all about. Within 45 minutes my coach had pulled me out of the hole I was in and taken me to a place where I felt there were options and that I had the power to change things.

I didn't know how she'd done it, all I knew was that she had asked me to physically move around my bedroom, sitting and standing in different positions, each one making me think and feel in a different way. Then I chose the one I wanted to go with and that was that. I literally *felt* different, *thought* differently, and had made a choice to get out of the place I was in, and *do* something to take back control of my life.

Although my journey from that point to this has been anything but plain sailing, coaching has helped me get in touch with

who I really am, what really matters to me, and design a life to make me feel happier and more fulfilled. It has helped me overcome my extreme workaholism (although I am a work-in-progress, as many of us are), helped me give up my heavy drinking and excessive shopping habit, challenged and shifted my major fears, doubts and insecurities, and helped me build a solid, stable life for me and my daughter. It has also helped me honour and live my life's purpose, which is to help others do the same.

Why I wrote this book

Over the past 12 years, I have worked with hundreds of clients who have also revealed how dissatisfied they are with their lives but who are convinced they don't have a choice, that they *have* to live like this (but can't bear it), that they need to stay in their job (but it's killing them inside), that they *can't* do what they dream of doing (it won't pay the bills), and are scared they will fail. They feel shame that they don't know how to get out of their situation. Many of them don't understand why they have ended up at this point, why they feel trapped without joy in their lives and no possible solution in sight. They have tried to change things, to make things better, but nothing has worked.

Don't let this be you. Don't wait until it's too late before you realize that you've wasted your one precious life – by doing a job you hate or not going for your dreams for fear you will fail. This is why I started my *Change Your Life in 5* video blog a couple of years ago and why I've written this book. I want as many people as possible to know that life doesn't have to be like this.

I want people to know about the information that is available – the tools and techniques I've learned along the way and use with my clients on a daily basis. These tools will help you to live your life from a true place of *conscious choice*. You won't learn these skills at school: how to live a value-lead life; how to best deal with fears, doubts and insecurities; how to choose how you respond to anything; how to take care of your mind body and spirit; how we all have a purpose – and what that is.

My purpose is to show you you always have a choice and you can always change things – even when you think you can't. It's what coaching has done for me and it's what I want for you. Judy Rich, the woman who blew my mind in 45 minutes, became my first coach and is now a very dear friend. In our early days of working together, she sent me a lovely card as encouragement during those tumultuous times. I have it up on my wall to this day, as a daily reminder: *She not only saw a light at the end of the tunnel, she became that light for others.*

Based on my own journey, extensive research and training, and just over a decade of working with clients, this book and the five core principles I have developed will guide you through a process of learning how to make *conscious* decisions and change *anything* in your life you are not happy with. I see my courageous clients doing this on a daily basis. I see them take step after step, stumble and fall, and then get up and carry on as they make new choices and take positive action. As one of my clients put it beautifully last week, 'I thought I didn't have a choice, but now I know I do.' And that's what I want for you too. My wish is that you use the

information in this book to help you start living your life from a true place of choice.

How to use this book

This book is structured around five core principles. Start with any chapter, depending on where you need the most guidance. If you feel completely stuck – then start with CLARIFY (what is really important to you and why you're here), then go straight to CHOOSE (to shift yourself away from where you are trapped). If you start with CLARIFY but feel that the focus on dreams is not for you, then go straight to CONQUER, to identify and deal with the beliefs that are preventing you from changing your life. If you are paralyzed by perfectionism or feeling not good enough, go straight to CELEBRATE. If you're exhausted and have no energy to spare, go straight to COMMIT (how to create the time and space needed to create change).

Making changes in your life is not a linear process – as individuals we each have our own blind spots and areas that need attention. Check in with where you are, and if you don't know, that's fine too.

When you have chosen a chapter, read it thoroughly, re-reading if necessary. Then create the time and space to do the exercises before moving onto the next chapter. Working through these exercises will ensure you get the most value out of this book. Any permanent, meaningful change requires increased self-awareness plus consistent action. That's why I have written the book in this format – to give you both the relevant psychological theory and brain science, plus the accompanying practical coaching exercises.

01

CLARIFY

From the Latin *clarus* meaning 'clear' or 'distinct';
to make coherent, easy to see, certain, definite.

Does your life feel meaningless? Are you often anxious? Do you feel disconnected from your loved ones? Do you feel stuck in a rut and is this having a negative impact on your mental health and general sense of wellbeing? Do you want to feel like this for the next 20, 30 or 40 years?

If you have forgotten what makes you really happy, what you want, and where you want to be in life, the first thing you need is *clarity*. This chapter is all about discovering why you are having these feelings and what to start doing to change them. It will give you the clarity that you need. It will help you identify and take time out to discover what's really important to you – which may not be exactly what you thought, and could even be a complete revelation. You will discover what's going on beneath the surface, and what to do to start changing things. You will identify your core values and your life's mission statement, and create a clear future, which will make you feel happy, satisfied, and more at peace.

IS THIS ALL THERE IS?

It's natural and normal to reflect on your life, and sometimes big life events such as key birthdays or milestones make you do this more, encouraging you to question what you're doing and why. Hopefully you feel pretty content and happy with where you are and where you're going. However, when you are forced to stop and think, a feeling of uneasiness can emerge. Have you ever asked yourself any of these questions: How did I end up here? What am I doing with my life? Is this all there is?

I've been coaching since 2008. Since then, every single one of my clients has said at least one of these things during our very first meeting. Either they've been feeling like this for a couple of years, or something big has happened in their life which has forced them to question everything.

They're usually at a point where circumstances seem to have come to a head, when they can no longer tolerate what their life or current situation has become, when they feel a bit lost or despondent, or they've lost their spark but don't really know why or what to do about it. They want more than

'this'; they feel their life has no meaning, but don't actually know what could bring them more of a sense of satisfaction and joy.

It's a scary place, and there doesn't seem to be any escape. Trust me. I know. I've been there. I had my daughter, Amelie, at the age of 34, and while initially it was great, and I took a whole year out, I did what many people do from that point onwards and had everything planned out: return to work, childcare arranged, done. Then I started to feel a real sense of, 'Uh-oh, this doesn't feel right', and what I actually started to want didn't fit with my previous plan. I vividly remember the day when it hit me like a proverbial sledgehammer to the head. I'd gone back to my job as a television producer and had been out filming reactions to the stabbing of a teenage boy. I'd got off the bus at the end of my road and was literally running to get back to Amelie; it was just turning 7pm. I walked into my flat and saw her there – on her nan's knee – all floppy and red. She'd been ill all day. I felt a huge visceral reaction, and I stood there in the doorway and thought, 'No, this isn't right; what am I doing?' But I didn't know what to do. I knew I didn't want 'this', I just didn't know what I did want or how I could possibly get there.

This is always how my clients feel when they come to coaching. They may present as wanting a new job, having to decide whether to go further up the career ladder or start their own business, whether to move to a new place etc., but underneath they all feel that the life they are living is just not right for them, but they have no idea what 'right' would look like. Not so far underneath the surface of their everyday lives, they feel confused, frustrated, bored, angry – and they just don't want to feel like that anymore.

IS THIS YOU?

- You've got it all, but you feel empty, unhappy and directionless.

- You've overachieved your whole life but are finding it hard to think about what comes next.

- You're going through the motions of living the life you've built, but you're no longer taking any joy from it.

- You don't feel like you've truly achieved your full potential.

THE WHEEL OF LIFE

Think about the different areas of your life, and give each one a rating out of ten for the amount of satisfaction you feel with it: 0 being completely dissatisfied, 10 being completely satisfied. Link up the sections by drawing a line to create a new outer edge and then answer the following questions.

Which areas need the most attention?

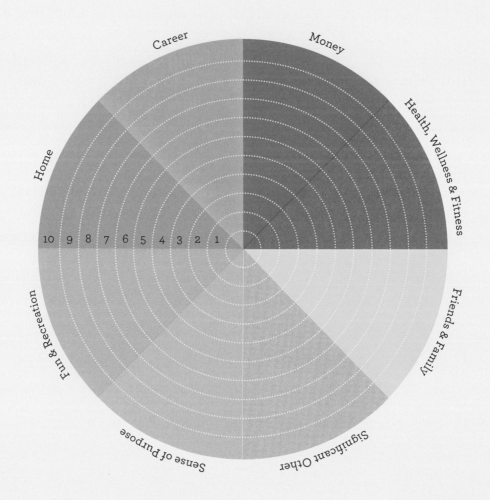

What does living like this cost you? For example,
being truly happy or quality time with your family.

Fast-forward five years. If you don't start changing
things now, where will you be?

When you are 80 or 90 years old and look back on your life, what do
you want to be able to say about how you lived it?

What is one thing you can do, this week, to improve the score of one
of the lowest-ranking sections? Make sure it is specific, measurable and
time-related. For example, 'This week I will go for two 30-minute walks in the woods'.

Most of my clients talk to me about one or more of the feelings outlined below. They are trapped in their own heads, bound up by fear, overburdened with responsibility, and feeling guilty and frustrated for not being able to think and plan their own way out of their current situation. They never feel present or at peace, and are unable to take a moment to enjoy the fruits of their hard work. Consider which of the following describe you:

01. Unhappy with your career

You used to be ambitious and innovative. Now, you hate your job, feel too old to move and are unfulfilled, but are too blocked and scared to control your own future. This book will help you discover what's happened and why, and what you can do about it.

02. Anxious and overwhelmed

On edge and struggling, you feel stuck, flat and lost. Sometimes a new bag, holiday or house will quell the fear, but it always comes back. You're a go-getting over-achiever; impatient about your inability to change your life for the better. In this book you'll uncover the fears, doubt and insecurities that are holding you back and will quickly, effectively and pragmatically set you on a new path.

03. Unfulfilled and empty

You wake up feeling there must be more to life than this, but think you've left it too late to fulfill your potential. Work consumes your time and energy: you're 100 per cent responsibility and 0 per cent contentment. Reading this book will give you clarity about what you want, so you can have the impact and make the contribution that you dream of.

04. Guilty

You've worked hard to achieve the career, relationship, maybe children, and the lifestyle you've always wanted. You just don't want it any more. You feel that you should be happy, and you try to be grateful and enjoy the fruits of your hard work, but you can't. Reading this book you will identify what you want in your life from now on and ensure you get it.

The conflict

Everything you are feeling is absolutely normal. Everything you are struggling with and feel hopeless about is a part of human psychological development. Psychologists refer to it as *individuation* (Carl Jung) or *self-actualization* (Abraham Maslow).

Whatever you want to call it, it amounts to the same thing: a drive or need to become

'A musician must make music, an artist must paint, a poet must write, if he is to be ultimately happy. What a man can be, he must be. This need we may call self-actualization.'

ABRAHAM MASLOW

our true selves – who we truly are when we are performing at our full potential, and using our own *natural* set of talents and abilities versus what we have been told or 'conditioned' to believe.

Jung believed that it's a natural drive within us – to want more meaning in life; Maslow believed it is a need that develops once our material needs have been met, when we naturally want to have more meaning and purpose in our lives. I believe it's a mixture of both – both a natural drive and something that happens when you have all of the things you've been striving for.

Take a look at Maslow's hierarchy of needs on the following page. This illustrates his idea that we all have certain basic needs, and fulfilling these helps us to thrive. He groups them into five levels; you have to fulfill the needs of one level before you can move up to the next.

The problem comes when the life we have, the life we have created and built for ourselves doesn't actually fit who we truly are – i.e. our *natural* talents and abilities. This is because up until a certain point (usually around the age of 35), we have designed our lives based on what we have been told we *should* be doing, *can't* do, or on only what is *possible* for us to do in life (in order to earn a living, support ourselves etc.).

This is all perfectly normal: we learn the 'rules of life' from who or what we see around us – parents, teachers, sometimes religion, society in general – but all of these have just been following the 'rules' that have been passed down to them. We follow these dictates in order to belong, to fit in, and to survive in the world as we know it. So, we enter careers that we have been led to believe are right for us, follow a path that has been laid out in front of us as 'the

SELF-ACTUALIZATION
Achieving one's full potential

SELF-ESTEEM
Prestige and feeling of accomplishment

SOCIAL BELONGING
Intimate relationships and friends

SAFETY NEEDS
Safety and security

PHYSIOLOGICAL NEEDS
Food, water, rest and good health

way', and even choose partners based on what we learn about relationships from our parents.

This is where the conflict or 'midlife crisis' comes in. The conflict happens when we find ourselves stuck between two worlds: the life we have created, but which no longer seems to fit or bring us any joy (let alone passion); and the yearning we have within us to actually follow our true path and calling in life – basically be who we were always meant to be.

If you don't know or understand what's going on beneath the surface, this is the point at which a sense or feeling of 'crisis' occurs. This is when you see people trying to 'fix' themselves to make themselves feel better, or trying to suppress their feelings of confusion and malaise by *external* means. This is the time at which people typically move house or area, leave their long-term partners (and yes often have affairs with a younger/more successful/better-looking version of their partner), or dive further into their careers – all in the hope that they might regain that sense of satisfaction and joy they once felt.

This is when we see the cliché of the middle-aged man buying a sports car or a motorbike, or suddenly taking up cycling (equipped of course with the latest bike and all the skin-tight cycling outfits). Men will strive to appear more youthful or more adventurous, or to look as if they are 'achieving' something – all to make themselves feel better about their lives.

Women will often begin to question their work and personal achievements, and start thinking about different ways of earning a living – typically starting businesses of their own or 'portfolio careers'. Women have more financial freedom now than ever before, and are therefore much less likely to 'put up and shut up' than previous generations. Statistics show that today's women are now less financially dependent on their partners, and are able to afford the kinds of life changes that were once only available to men (about 25 per cent of wives today earn more than their husbands). Women are also now *almost* as likely as men to have affairs, and two out of every three divorces are now initiated by women. So when faced with the question, 'How do you really want your life to be?', women are now much more likely to make a radical change and move on.

Waking up

I think it's time to rebrand the 'midlife crisis'. I like to call it 'waking up', and I see this as a completely positive life stage to go through. Or rather it *can* be. If you know what's going on under the surface. If you use this time in your life to question, re-evaluate, and do some challenging work around redesigning your life the way you *really* want it to be, you will get to enjoy many more fulfilling years.

This is when people come to me for coaching. My guess is that this is why you are reading this book. You know that things just don't feel right, your unhappy and you just don't know what you *do* want, or you do know deep down, but just don't feel it's possible.

Well, I'm here to tell you the same thing I tell all of my clients – whatever you truly want (even if you don't know what that is right now), *is* possible. Not only is it possible, you can have it. It will take some serious questioning, a lot of courage, and some hard work to get you from where you are now to the place that will make you feel truly happy, satisfied and fulfilled, but trust me, it's worth it.

You only have to look around you to see the effects on people who have not faced up to these questions and actually taken action.

It takes a lot of courage and hard work to face up to the big questions at this stage in your life. If you do not listen to the questions, thoughts and reflections you are now experiencing and which have encouraged you to read this book – you will be faced with many decades of regret, resentment, boredom and anger.

An incredible book that brings this point home is *The Top Five Regrets of the Dying: A Life Transformed by the Dearly Departing* by Bronnie Ware. Bronnie is a nurse who worked in palliative care for several years and wrote about what she learned from working with her patients. She undertook a series of interviews with patients and went on to compile a list of their top five regrets:

01. I wish I'd had the courage to live a life true to myself, not the life others expected of me.
02. I wish I hadn't worked so hard, and so much.
03. I wish I'd had the courage to express my feelings more.
04. I wish I'd been better at staying in touch with my friends.
05. I wish that I had let myself be happier.

Wow, what a list. The one that hit me the most the first time I read it was number two: 'I wish I hadn't worked so hard, and so much.' This is something I am working on at the moment, as it is a regret I definitely do not want to feel on my deathbed, and one that I know I will if I don't take action. I have struggled with this for a long time and am now consciously working fewer hours, taking more time to relax and enjoy life, and spending a lot more time with friends and family. I have turned off almost all the app notifications on my phone; I am taking more time out to do fun things with my daughter (rather than fitting in 'just one more hour of work'); and also forcing myself to take more rest days and to spend more time, out in nature, with my boyfriend and friends. How about you?

You can absolutely change your future. You do not need to be one of those people with the regrets listed on the previous pages – you do have a choice. It's *my* life purpose to show you that there is a different way to live, and that it can be exactly how you want it to be.

To change your life will take great courage and hard work, but with this awareness, together with the positive actions that this book suggests, you can start designing the life you were meant to live. If you completed the exercise on pages 18–21, you have already made a start).

If you don't yet know what your 'ideal life' actually looks like, then read on so you can start to clarify now.

Your ideal life

You only get one life. This is it. Seriously, I think this vitally important fact becomes lost in the reality and grind of everyday life. Whatever your religious or spiritual beliefs, this is the only life you have right now.

Take a moment to ask yourself the following questions: Is what you are doing right now, and the path you're on, *it* for you? Is what you are doing right now fulfilling? Does your life bring you joy? Are you living the dreams and goals you had as a teenager or in your early 20s; has it all panned out as you imagined? My guess is not, and my guess is, as you're reading this book, that deep down you know there must be more, or at least you *hope* there is. Even on a day-to-day basis – is this really how you want to be living your life – for the next 20, 30 or 40 years?

THE REGRET BUSTER

Looking at the list on page 26, write down the regrets you do not want to have, or think of and write down your own.

What are the things you will do to start busting these regrets now?

FULFILLMENT

I trained with the Co-Active Training Institute (CTI) and one of their core principles is *fulfillment*. They believe that we all have a yearning for something deeper – a fulfilling life with meaning, purpose and satisfaction. How does that sound to you? Possible? Far-off? Does this apply to what you are doing with *your* life? And most importantly, why would you not want that?

Why would you not want to feel, all the time, deep down, a sense of being whole, alive, and satisfied – for the rest of your life? That is what this book is all about and what I want for you, because that's my version of a fulfilling life.

Normally, most of us just focus on what we have or don't have – the 'things' that give us momentary pleasure, such as the shiny new car that makes us feel good for about six months, and then loses its appeal, and so on to the next thing and the next. I'm not saying there's anything wrong with wanting 'things' – the car, a nice house, a successful career, a great relationship. What I'm saying is, don't assume they will make you feel fundamentally satisfied at any deep level, or for any long period of time.

Feeling 'good' isn't a sign of living a fulfilled life either. Leading a fulfilling life can give you a deep sense of peace and ease, but it can also feel like a struggle. Living a life of purpose and meaning can be the more difficult route to take but it is really worth it, because on the inside you will feel a deeper sense of satisfaction, and know that you're doing what is right for you.

What I have learned is this: our outer worlds truly are a direct reflection of our inner worlds and whatever we believe, will be.

Your version of fulfillment

Most people out there in the world are walking around, going about their daily lives without knowing what it is that would truly 'fulfill' them. This stuff doesn't get taught in schools. We are all so busy just getting by, dealing with the next problem, meeting the next deadline, going for the next promotion, that there is no time to actually stop and ask these questions – or if we do, it feels far too frightening because we don't have the answers (or rather, we think we don't).

What we do is buy another dress, another car, a bigger house, change our partner for a shiny new one – all in the hope that these 'things' will get rid of that gnawing anxiety deep down inside. That anxiety is a direct result of us not fulfilling our true potential, or even identifying what that might be.

We are so conditioned from a very early age (in fact since birth) to think, behave, and believe in a certain way – what we *can* do, *can't* do, *should* do, *have* to do, *don't dare* do or be – in accordance with what others think and believe *is* possible for us (and what they were told was possible for them). So it's no wonder that you've not had a chance (so far) to sit down and ask what your vision of a really fulfilling life looks like. Sometimes it's not all that fantastical.

A couple of weeks ago, a new client came to me because she had been living very 'small' for her entire adult life – her words not mine. What she really wanted, and why she was coming to me, was to 'live an expanded life and get the confidence to start dating'. She was 36 years old and had been living a life that involved work, having a few drinks after work, and then going home – literally for 15 years. I asked her to visualize her ideal world and to really dare to dream. It took a good while to move her away from what she thought was or wasn't possible, but when she did, all she actually wanted was a slightly fuller life – to live in a town centre flat to feel more connected, to live with a partner, and to have a vibrant social life where again she felt more engaged with others and the world in general. That was it and it was all possible! She had just, up to that point, not dared to imagine it – so how on earth could she have made it happen?

Indeed, what all my clients over the years, and I, have truly wanted, hasn't actually been that far out of reach either – it just feels that way. It feels impossible – so impossible in fact, that we feel we can't go there.

Deep down you do know what you want your life to look like and you know exactly what brings you joy and fulfillment. I see clients every day who have built their whole lives around what they were told was or wasn't possible for them, and yet deep down they feel bored, unsatisfied and unfulfilled. This is normal. What you are experiencing is normal.

Dare to dream

In order for you to really find out what you truly want, you are going to have to put conditioning and fear to one side. You are going to have to *dare* to *dream*. This is your one time to fantasize and to create your ideal world scenario – what do you want your life to look like?'

I know that already there will be a sabotaging voice in your head saying, 'But that's not possible/I can't have that/I'm not qualified to do that/I don't know anything about that … etc,.' I'm not diminishing what this voice is saying, I just want you to notice this voice right now, know it isn't actually yours (although it feels like it), it's one of the ones you've picked up along the way, and I want you to set it aside/put it away or whatever you need to do to not let it limit you. That's what it's been doing all your life, and my guess is it's no longer serving you – which is the number one reason you're not already living your 'dream' life. The check-in question to ask every time this voice pops up is, 'How is it serving me to listen to this?', and if it isn't – don't! If you really can't set this voice aside at the moment, if it really will not let you even dare to dream, just for a moment, then please pause here and go straight to Chapter two, Conquer, and then come back.

What would my life look like if I believed anything is possible?

What will most certainly happen as you go through this process, and what always happens with my clients as I am taking them through this exercise, is that even if you can get past those voices to start the exercise, you will keep going back to what you currently think is possible, or what can be achieved within the constraints of money, time and resources.

Every time this happens, keep pulling yourself back to your vision. Keep thinking about your ideal world scenario of how you would love your life to look. View this as your time to completely dream big, fantasize. You'll be surprised. When I ask clients to do this, and they ask, 'What, really dream, really – what's not really possible?' and they do go there and discover what they want, like the client I mentioned earlier, isn't that fantastical at all – only to them. This is because they have become so used to the sabotaging voices *saying* it's not

'Fulfillment is the state of fully expressing who we are and doing what is right for us ... wholeness, satisfaction, a sense of rightness and harmony ... everything we most value is in alignment ... The pieces of (our) lives or careers come together in a very personal sense of wholeness and of feeling very alive.'

HENRY KIMSEY-HOUSE, KAREN KIMSEY-HOUSE, PHILLIP SANDAHL & LAURA WHITWORTH

possible and what they want really isn't unattainable: living in a lovely cottage by the sea; having a caring partner; running their own business doing something they're actually passionate about. This is all completely doable – it just seems out of reach for *them*.

As a result of how we have been conditioned, we are all convinced that we can only do, have and be certain ways and things. Let me tell you, this is the biggest hurdle you have to jump – getting beyond these limiting beliefs. How would it be, what would your life look like if, instead of believing everything you had been told, you actually believed 'Anything *is* possible'?

DARE TO DREAM

Find a quiet space, somewhere completely private, where you won't get interrupted. Start by reading through the following questions. Stop and think about them for about 10 minutes (set a timer on your phone if that's helpful). Then, stand up, move around, shake out your arms and legs and then settle at a point in the room. Studies by neuroscientists have shown that moving our bodies allows our brain to open up and think in different, more expanded ways. Now, close your eyes and imagine yourself in exactly two years' time. Open your eyes and answer the questions as fully as you can.

What does your life look like?

If time and resources were not a concern what would you be doing?

Where would you be living?

What does your home, feel, sound and smell like?

Who would you be sharing your life with?

What would your daily routine consist of?

Where would you be working?

YOUR VALUES

By imagining your ideal life – the things that would bring you joy, satisfaction and use your full potential – you have described a life that reflects what you *value* most. Values are what is most important to you, what you most care about, what makes you tick. This is important, because when we are living a life according to our values, we are leading a truly fulfilling life and feel an internal sense of 'rightness'.

Conversely, when we are living a life that *dishonours* those values – ignoring them, doing the opposite of what's right for us (remember all the conditioning that causes this to happen?), then we feel things are 'not right' – something that is known as 'dissonance', an inner sense of *dis*harmony

When this goes on for a long time, or our values are dishonoured to extremes, anxiety, depression, anger, and potentially physical illness can result. This is when clients come to me – when they feel a high degree of dissonance, and when they've had enough of feeling like this. They've typically tried several of the quick fixes I've already talked about, but none of them

have worked, and their sense of unease has only increased.

When I did my coaching training in 2008 with CTI, clarifying my values was a huge revelation to me. It was also a bit of a shock, as it made me realize how my life wasn't honouring my values and why I felt so lost and unhappy. My top values are: deep connection; learning, growth and discovery; freedom; nurture and altruism; beauty and excellence.

Of course, I didn't even know what a value was back in my 'previous life' as I call it. Reading this list out now explains my negative feelings about my life and work as a television producer.

'I have learned that as long as I hold fast to my beliefs and values – and follow my own moral compass – then the only expectations I need to live up to are my own.'

MICHELLE OBAMA

Having started out as a local news reporter, I went on to produce many different documentaries. I absolutely loved my job, and looking back at what I now know to be my values, I can see that my job was helping me to live most of them. I loved going into new environments and finding out about how they worked and the people that lived in them (learning, growth and discovery); I loved meeting those people and encouraging them to share their stories (deep connection); and I really enjoyed the rest of the process of filming and piecing programmes together to create a story to be shared with others (beauty and excellence).

However, I began to have problems with other parts of the programme-making process and what I did for a living. I worked on some programmes where the subject matter and the experiences I asked people to talk about on camera were very challenging: I was hearing stories about sexual abuse, drug addiction, rape, domestic abuse, suicide and even murder.

I started to struggle with the lack of aftercare offered to these people (nurture value), who we asked to share their innermost thoughts, feelings and heartache, and then just left them to it – as well as broadcasting their suffering to millions of people. Yes, they had agreed to all this, and yes, in many cases the experience of talking was a cathartic one. However, when the cameras stopped rolling, we literally packed up and left those people with everything they had just disclosed. I vividly remember having interviewed a woman about the murder of her teenage son in a gang fight on her housing estate. I really felt her pain; it had a visceral effect on me. At the end of the interview I wanted to help her and said, 'Let me know If you ever need anything,' and she said, 'Like what?' Exactly – like what? There really wasn't anything I could do – and for me that was the problem. I did not feel I was taking care of her in that situation and this did not square with my core value of nurture and altruism – I felt like I'd got what I wanted and I was just leaving.

VALUES CLARIFICATION

Set aside some time and space, and answer the following questions. Really take time out to do this; you will also benefit from doing it once, thinking about it, and then going back and fleshing it out further.

Look forward 20 years. You are attending a function where someone is giving a speech about you. What would you want them to say?

If time and resources were not a concern, describe the things you long to do.

Think about one or two people you know who really inspire you.
What about them is inspiring?

What's missing in your life, the presence of which would make your life more fulfilling?

What activities have heart and meaning for you?

What activities energise you?

What needs in the world are you moved to meet?

What drives you crazy?

Once you've answered the questions on the previous pages as fully as possible, review what you've written. Referring to the list of words on pages 46–47, ask yourself and note down the 10 words that resonate most with you. For example, painting, drawing, writing would mean creativity is a strong value for you.

Using this list go back to your ideal life visualization notes and see which of the same values you can also spot there. Write them down here.

Using the list of words on the following pages, circle others
that feel very important to you.

Place your 10 values in order of priority (1 being not honouring at all,
10 being fully honouring this value) and score each one out of 10
according to whether your current life is reflecting them.

Write down which values you are honouring and which values
you are dishonouring.

Contribution/Service

Recognition

Tradition

Time & Space

Peace

Respect

Excellence

Fun

Integrity

Community

Freedom

Joy

Adventure

Wisdom

Authenticity

Challenge

Accuracy

Directness

Choice

Orderliness

Harmony

Creativity

Connection

Safety/Security

Aesthetics & Beauty

Full Self-Expression

Curiosity

Altruism

Honesty

Achievement

Collaboration

Independence

Humour

Learning, Growth & Discovery

Spirituality

Responsibility

Vitality

Health & Wellbeing

Connection with Nature

Excellence/Accuracy

Trust

YOUR PURPOSE

The other key to unlocking a deep sense of 'rightness' in your life is discovering your 'purpose'. By this I mean what you are here to do, why you are here and the nature of your contribution to the world. We all have a purpose, we all have a unique contribution to make to this world, at this time.

When I talk to people about this, they always ask: 'What, you really believe we all have a purpose, we are all here for a reason?' Yes I do!

Using your individual talents and having lived your specific life journey, you have a unique bank of knowledge and wisdom to bring to others. When you discover your purpose, you will know that too – you will feel it. What's great about identifying your purpose and knowing what it is, is that, just like your values, it can act as a compass in your life and as a yardstick by which to measure anything that you are doing or thinking about doing. It enables you to ask the question: 'How is this supporting my life purpose?' Just like living a life honouring your values, staying true to your purpose is

not always the easiest path but it will lead you to a richer and more fufilling life.

If living a life honouring our values and living out our purpose is so great, you may ask, why we are not all doing it already? For me, and all of my clients, the main reason has always been that fear is much stronger than the desire for fulfillment. This is the fear I described earlier. The fear that leads to self-sabotage, that comes in a variety of forms and creates a feeling of *dissonance* within us. It can come in the form of frustration, boredom, anger or indifference. When clients come and meet me for the first time, I can sense it as they sit there and tell me why they *'can't'* have the life they want, why they *'need'* to be doing what they're doing, how they're not *'good/smart/*

experienced/wealthy enough' or '*too old/ young/stupid/*' to have the life they really want. We'll go into this in more detail in the next chapter, but just know for now that we all have these voices, and for all of us they have run out of control and have started running the show – the show that is your life.

Through identifying their life's purpose, I have seen clients completely shift how they feel about themselves, their careers and their lives. I have seen them go from a place where they are just trudging along, feeling pretty lost and uninspired and questioning what on earth they are doing (even to the point of giving everything up and starting again), to a place where they have a real mission, true meaning and

satisfaction, and where they are making a difference and a real contribution to the world.

One client I worked with recently is a classic case in point. She had been identified as a 'rising star', someone in her industry with 'high potential'. She was earmarked for great things, had worked her way up, been very successful, had a great salary, good prospects, the lot, but when she came to me she said, 'I just wake up in the morning and wonder what I'm doing. Why am I doing it all? What's it all for?' She was at a complete loss as to why she felt like this and what to do about it, and felt completely trapped by the weight of her work and family responsibilities – she had a husband, two children and a mortgage to pay.

'Finding and claiming a life purpose gives clients a powerful sense of direction in their lives. The truth they find in the life purpose statement can make them virtually unstoppable.'

HENRY KIMSEY-HOUSE, KAREN KIMSEY-HOUSE,
PHILLIP SANDAHL & LAURA WHITWORTH

By gaining clarity about her life purpose, she discovered that she wanted to make a big difference in her industry to how people were treated, to working conditions in general, and specifically to equality for women within the workplace. She wanted to leave the industry in a better place than it was when she joined. She is now very active in bringing those changes about, has become a spokesperson for creating those changes, and inspires others to speak out and share their experiences. She is making a real difference. Now she gets out of bed with a spring in her step and knows exactly why she's there.

As Simon Sinek, author of the global bestseller *Start With Why* says: 'Working hard for something we don't care about is called stress. Working hard for something we love is called passion ... Our actions should start with WHY not WHAT.'

The fact that you are even reading this book is a result of me having identified my life purpose. I didn't know it at the time, but the reason I first went into television was because I had a deep yearning to share people's stories. Underneath that, as I now know, is my purpose: I want people to know there is a different way to live and I love sharing the information and tools that show people they always have a choice, and can change things – even when they think they can't.

It was only when I did the Co-Active Training Institute exercise on the following pages that I discovered this was the purpose underlying what I had been doing all those years and why, ultimately what I was doing and how the industry had evolved and worked was not actually honouring my purpose or values. Discovering my purpose has also allowed me to help hundreds of clients discover, and live by their own values – and this is what I want for you.

YOUR LIFE PURPOSE

These guided visualizations and subsequent questions will help you start to formulate your own life purpose or mission statement. As before, create some private time and space for this. Between each of the visualizations, once you have a full, rich image, open your eyes and jot down your answers.

Guided inner journey 1

Think of a time in your life when you felt at your most powerful – a time when your spine, arms and fingertips were tingling with excitement, a time when you simply didn't care what anyone thought of you. You were absolutely alive. Notice where you were, what you were doing and who was around you. Write down the answers to the following questions.

Where were you?

What were you doing?

Who was around you?

Guided inner journey 2

You've been given a billboard and can put any message you want on it. Thousands of people will drive by and see your billboard every day.

What does it say?

Guided inner journey 3

You are getting into a spaceship. The spaceship takes off. You are on your way to an undeveloped planet in the universe. It's a fine planet in every way, but it's uninhabited. You have the power to make this planet whatever you want it to be. When you land, what is it that you're going to make happen: what's the impact you want to have, that's going to create the planet in the way you want it to be?

The ship is landing. The doors open. You touch the planet and say, 'It's going to be this way.' What is 'this way'?

Once you have done all of these visualizations and written down what came from each one, go back and look for all of the impact words and themes that come up. For example, for me, I wanted people to have choice and feel free, and my billboard said, 'You always have a choice.' Now, hone that down to create the beginnings of your life purpose statement:

I am here to ...

CONQUER

From the Latin *conquirere* meaning to 'gain, or 'win';
to successfully overcome, take control of.

What would you do if you knew you could not fail? What would you do if you weren't so afraid? What would you do if you didn't care what people thought?

This chapter is all about revealing the fears that are stopping you from living the life of your dreams. You will discover where they come from, the identity of the voice in your head that is sabotaging your dreams, why it is so powerful and how to stop it holding you back.

You will also uncover your biggest ally against fear: your Future Self – your older, wiser self who is living a life of purpose and fulfillment. You will learn how to start using your Future Self as a wise guide that you can use to steer you in the right direction. Whenever you need to know what your next step should be, you can tap into this inner source of wisdom – something that is especially helpful when facing down your fears and overcoming sabotaging voices.

FEAR

Sometimes late at night you may think about the life you wish you had – the job that got away (you were too scared to apply); that holiday or trip of a lifetime you haven't made yet, or those abandoned health kicks, exercise programmes, hobbies and friends. Fear is telling you that if you try to achieve that life, you will lose everything you already have … you can't … you'll fail. So, you don't. Fear can stop you from having a rich, fulfilling life.

We are all hard-wired to feel fear, it is a normal part of brain function and we actually need it to survive. When we face an unknown, or a perceived threat, the oldest part of our brain is triggered – the limbic system, most notably the amygdala. The amygdala is an almond-shaped section of nervous tissue located deep in the temporal lobe of the brain. Research has shown that it performs a primary role in the processing of memory, decision-making and emotional responses (including fear, anxiety, and aggression).

When triggered by a 'stressful stimulus' – an unknown outcome or danger – the amygdala sets off a chain reaction that ends with the release of chemicals that cause a racing heart, fast breathing and primed muscles, among other things. This is known as the 'fight-flight-freeze' response, and prepares you to tackle (the predator), run and hide, or play dead. Our fears fall into three main categories:

01. Natural instinct
These are the natural fears we're born with and that keep us alive, e.g. fear of heights (so we don't fall off cliffs), pain (so we don't hurt or kill ourselves), and loud noises (often a sign of impending danger).

02. Learned from experience
These are the fears of places, situations or

people. For example, I have recently been conquering my fear of being in the sea – a fear I developed after nearly drowning in the sea when I was eight years old.

03. Taught by others

These are fears of risk, perceived harm and danger, fear of certain people or of things that will cause us to be rejected by others – all taught to us by our parents, teachers, society, religion, and prevailing culture. This is the main source of fear we will be focusing on in this book as it's the main source I see in people *not* living their ideal lives.

Whatever type of fear it is, *all* fears are partly imagined. This is because our brains are so hard-wired to protect us from danger that we may fear things that aren't *actually* a threat – and often don't even exist or haven't happened yet. We are often *imagining* things that *could* happen. And because of this well-developed ability to learn, imagine and even *create* fear in our own minds, some neuroscientists say that we are the most fearful creatures in the world.

Fear can run your life

Imagining what could happen based on what we have been taught by others (both explicitly and implicitly by how they live

their lives), is the real killer of dreams and lives. In my decade of practice, this kind of fear is the single main reason why clients are not living the life they really want, and feel so unhappy. Fear, unfortunately, is much stronger than our desire for fulfillment. Whether it's changing careers, leaving a relationship, moving house, changing our lifestyle, even changing our diet or fitness regime, we all have a fear of change. We are all afraid when faced with a situation where we don't know the outcome, or predict the outcome as presenting a danger to our survival.

I have heard clients say they are not living their ideal life because they are scared: of losing their home; losing whatever else they have built up for themselves; upsetting the status quo; upsetting loved ones; being made fun of or appearing ridiculous; failing; succeeding; making the wrong choices; relinquishing control: not knowing what the outcome might be; being rejected; being seen as a bad mother, bad daughter, or just plain 'selfish'; being found out as a fraud. All of these fears can have a huge impact on your life and how you live it (or don't fully live it).

In her book, *The Fear Cure*, Dr Lissa Rankin lists the 10 signs that fear is running your life as follows:

01. You find yourself striving in vain for an impossible-to-achieve standard of perfectionism.
02. You settle.
03. You say yes when you mean no.
04. You say no when you mean yes.
05. You numb yourself with alcohol, drugs, sex, television, or excessive busy-ness.
06. You procrastinate.
07. You get paralyzed.
08. You become a control freak.
09. You don't speak up for yourself.
10. You get ill.

Fearful people are said to be more likely to suffer from heart attacks, cancer, diabetes, autoimmune diseases, inflammatory disorders, chronic pain, as well as milder symptoms such as insomnia, fatigue, obesity, headaches, backaches, decreased libido and gastrointestinal distress.

Another sobering list don't you think? I certainly am prone to perfectionism and the numbing behaviour of 'busy-ness'. So, know that you are not alone, we all feel fear.

I get so annoyed when I see those 'be fearless' images and platitudes on social media. They are dangerous and make us feel worse about ourselves than we already do – because underneath we all feel scared. Those images just pile on the shame for feeling scared, when others seemingly don't. Whatever anyone tells you, and yes that includes the fearless brigade, they are scared too. They may pretend they're not – they may even be fearless about one thing but are actually very scared of another – but trust me, there is no way they are 100 per cent fearless about everything.

Hidden fears

There are people who seem to have overcome fear entirely – who do appear 'fearless'. They have achieved great things, built huge empires, succeeded in their fields, and look like they have it all. I work with these people on a daily basis and I can tell you this: most of them are also driven by fear. This is the fear of not being 'good enough' and therefore needing to constantly prove themselves and constantly chase the next big achievement. Everything they do only provides a temporary sense of satisfaction, until they feel the fear again and off they go to create the next thing that will subdue it – for a while. This is certainly something that has driven my life and that I continue to work on to this day. In the process of proving themselves to be 'worthy', these people nearly kill themselves. Everyone – these people included – would benefit from identifying the fear and living more from a place of choice and true fulfillment. Because there is another way to live.

Fear as protection

This is what fear can feel like – that it is is keeping you safe. It can feel as if fear is protecting us from danger, from losing everything we have, and that it is actually keeping us safe from harm. I'm talking about the voice in your head that says:

'What if I get rejected?'
'What if I fail?'
'What if I don't get it right/perfect?'
'What if I do X, and Y happens?'

The problem is that this voice keeps us *too* safe. It is designed to stop us from doing reckless things. It makes us overcautious and means we don't take any risks and we never have a fulfilling life. It keeps us small.

How to conquer fear

Fear will never go away. The only way to conquer the fear is to accept it and then do the thing you're afraid of. Scientists have shown that this is the only way to overcome fear – be proactive and face it – because every time you do and you physically survive, your brain is learning that there is no real threat after all. If you understand and crack this one, trust me, you really will be able to have the life you've only ever dreamed about. What you can learn to do, and what I hugely advocate, is the 'fake-it-till-you-make-it' approach or 'feel the fear and do it any way' – the title of the international bestseller, originally published in 1987 by psychologist Susan Jeffers. In the book, Jeffers talks about how fear limited her life and how the only way to deal with fear is to accept it, and then have the courage to do the thing that scares you. She discusses how fear is based on the uncertainty of change and the lack of positive self-image. She explains that the fundamental cause of fear is a lack of trust in oneself, the belief that 'I can't handle it!' As she puts it: 'We fear beginnings; we fear endings. We fear changing; we fear "staying stuck". We fear success; we fear failure. We fear living; we fear dying.' Her solution is to start learning to trust, replacing the fear of not surviving with the attitude that whatever happens, you can, and will, handle it.

You can see that in conquering your fears there is a lot for you to battle against, and it is absolutely possible to do so. As ever, the key is both an awareness of what's going on, and taking action to start changing things. You can begin right now.

WHAT FEAR IS GETTING IN YOUR WAY?

What would you do in and with your life if you weren't afraid? If you knew you couldn't fail? If time and resources weren't an issue? If you didn't care what people thought of you? Take some time out and answer the questions below.

What would you like to do?

Run my own furniture restoration business.

01.

02.

03.

04.

05.

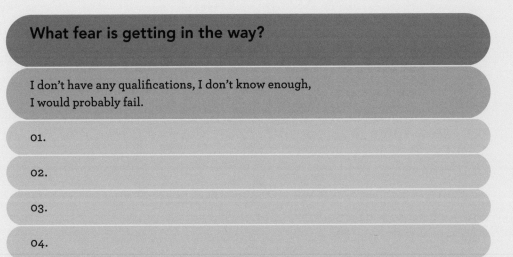

What fear is getting in the way?

I don't have any qualifications, I don't know enough,
I would probably fail.

01.

02.

03.

04.

05.

Now, choosing one of these fears, what is one (small, regular) action you could take to face it? Note that I have said small and regular. This is because when making any change, neuroscientists have shown that it is best to make a change that is as small and unscary as possible. Then, once that small change has been processed by the amygdala (and your brain catches up and learns that it won't kill you), you can incrementally increase the change, but keep as many other variables as possible (such as new locations, new times) the same as before – thereby reducing your overall fear levels.

SELF-SABOTAGING VOICES

In the first few years of our lives, we learn the 'rules' of how to behave and think in a way that allows us to survive. This is the time when we learn what we should do, what we can't do, what we have to do, in order to be accepted, loved, to belong, and to receive all the things we need to survive as a human being in this world.

The problems come if we reach a point in our lives when these beliefs no longer seem to 'fit' us any more – they no longer seem to be working well for us and only seem to be keeping us in a career that no longer gives us joy, in a relationship that we're no longer committed to, or just makes us feel generally unsatisfied and unfulfilled. What's happening is that at some point we begin to see glimpses of who we truly are and what we truly want – either because we are made to take a long hard look at our lives due to a forced change in circumstance, e.g. redundancy or having a child (as in my case), or because of a combination of things. However, these glimpses are pushed back by the voices in our heads that are now so strong and have become such an integral part of us, that having/doing/being what we truly want just seems impossible and out of our reach, leaving us feeling sad and generally disenchanted.

What is happening and why now?

This sense that our life no longer 'fits' can develop at a point when we are forced to question the meaning or purpose of everything in our life – often following traumatic events or illnesses. Up until then we've spent most of our lives meeting or having our needs met in terms of survival and safety, love and belonging, respect and recognition. We've been living our lives according to the voices in our heads that say, 'You've got to work hard', 'Security is the most important thing – don't risk all that to go and chase some silly dream', 'Don't get noticed, keep your head down and your nose to the grindstone'. These voices may have helped you build a pretty good and solid life for yourself, a good career, gain a lovely house or flat, a great circle of friends, a relationship and children.

However, these limiting beliefs, or 'sabotaging voices' as I learned about them with CTI, are not yours. They never were. They have been absorbed and passed down unconsciously from generation to generation. For example, I was brought up in an army family. My father was a sergeant major and my mother worked part-time, mainly in shops on the army bases. As you can imagine, a sergeant major in the army has a strong presence and some firmly held beliefs. As my father's daughter, I naturally learned and absorbed lots of his opinions and ways of getting by in the world. Many of these have served me very well (I am rarely late, extremely organized and goal-oriented – basically I get stuff done), but some were holding me back from living the life I really wanted to be living. There was nothing wrong with my father's way of living, it was just not right for me.

Psychologists say these self-sabotaging voices can also develop as a result of not having our needs met at different life stages. There are various different psychological models that describe these stages, but in his book *What My Soul Told Me*, Richard Barrett lists them as: Surviving, Conforming, and Differentiating.

The surviving stage

Barrett states that when we are a baby in the 'Surviving' stage and completely dependent on others, literally for our survival, we learn how to gain control to get our needs for food, shelter and affection met. If we are not able to – for example, if our parents aren't responsive enough, or we are left for long periods of time – we are likely to develop fear-based beliefs that the world is not a safe place and people can't be trusted.

The conforming stage

In the next 'Conforming' stage, as a young child, we learn that life is better and less threatening if we get along with those around us, and therefore 'belong' – to a family, a school culture, a religion, etc. This is when we're likely to take on those firmly held fears, beliefs and rules about how things are done or not done within a group.

The differentiating stage

During the 'Differentiating' stage (when we are teenagers), we need to feel special and different. It's absolutely vital that we get praise and recognition of our successes from our parents or primary caregivers. If we don't we will develop the subconscious, fear-based belief that we are just 'not good enough', which again develops into a sabotaging voice. This will be discussed more fully in Chapter 4.

The important thing to remember here is that, in general, these 'rules of life' aren't passed on with any malice (although sometimes I'm afraid this is not the case – more on this later) – they are passed on unconsciously with the intention of keeping you safe and supporting you on your potentially treacherous journey through the world.

You may have started questioning the fit and purpose of your life now because you've starting to realize that maybe, just maybe,

you've had it wrong all these years. You start to dream about what life might be like – if only you were free of the big mortgage, or you'd studied your passion (art, instead of accounting, for example, like one of my clients, whose father told them that there was 'No money in art' and that accounting would give them a stable, long-term career with a good income).

You are now experiencing moments of connection with your true self – who you really are underneath all of that 'conditioning'. Your soul or spirit (whatever you want to call your 'true self'), is rising up inside you and challenging everything that has gone before – by which I mean all of your survival techniques and the parts of your 'personality' you've developed to survive in the world. Your true self is saying, 'Hey, this isn't it for you, there is more', but the problem is that the other voices are so strong, and the circumstances you've created in your life are so reliant on you maintaining the status quo, that any other way of doing things just seems impossible – and really, really scary!

As I mentioned in Chapter 1, psychologists call this stage in our lives 'self-actualization'. This term basically describes a process through which you are getting to know who you truly are, what's

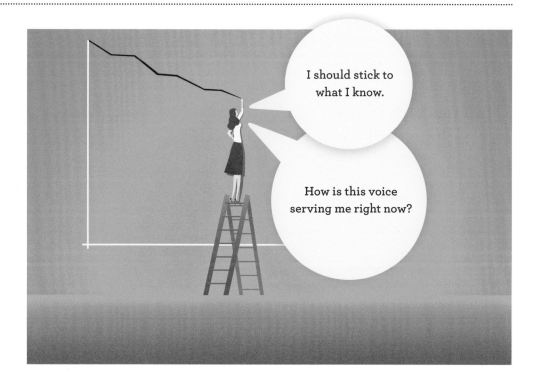

really important to you, and what your purpose is (yes, I believe everyone has a purpose). For me, this is where coaching comes in, as it can help you get in touch with who you really are, and what you really want your life to be like. This may sound easy, but when you've been living a life according to everyone else's rules, it takes a lot of courage, and a lot of hard work to get there.

During my time as a coach, the single most common sabotaging voice is that of my clients' mothers (followed closely by fathers, then various uncles, aunties,

grandparents, and even school teachers). Time and time again, when a new client walks through my door for the first time, and I ask them to tell me how they really want their life to be (remember that ideal world scenario?), up she pops saying, 'You should stick to what you know', 'People won't take you seriously', 'But what if you fail?' In actual fact, the first time I hear my client's sabotaging voice speak, nine times out of ten, when I explain the theory of saboteurs and ask if the voice reminds them of anyone, they instantly say, 'Oh yes, my mother!'.

'Inaction breeds doubt and fear. Action breeds confidence and courage. If you want to conquer fear, do not sit at home and think about it. Go out and get busy.'

DALE CARNEGIE

I have become quite the 'saboteur sniffer' over the years and can sense the insidious voice of a saboteur on my first meeting with a client. It shows up in their apparently convincing justifications as to why their dream life just isn't possible for them – from the 'Oh, I'll do it when I'm retired as I'll have the time and won't need to earn so much money then', to the 'I couldn't set up my own business as I just don't have the time/experience/knowledge' and the more obvious, 'I'm not talented/smart/experienced enough' ... and so on.

How to stop the voices running your life

Let me reassure you straight away – you can get hold of these voices and stop them running the show. That's the good news; the not-so-great news is that it's not a quick fix, and it takes a lot of work. Just being aware of the voices is the first step. The next one is to give them an identity, and then every time you hear them saying, 'You can't/should/have to ...', assign that voice to the person it came from, and then send them off.

This is what is possible if you can get hold of that voice, separate it out, and stop it controlling and limiting your life. It's not completely black and white I know – this voice has probably kept you safe for a certain period. A great check-in question to ask when you're not sure if it's a good idea to listen to the voice or not when you really can't work out if it's helping or hindering you to get the life you want – is to ask yourself: 'How is it serving me to listen to this voice right now?' If it's not, you have a choice: be a victim (or a martyr because you are not making a real choice and then complaining about it), or take a stand for yourself and your life. Which will you choose?

IDENTIFY YOUR SABOTEUR

Answer the following questions to identify the main sabotaging voice that's preventing you from living your ideal life.

Imagine your ideal life. Make a list of the phrases that pop up into your head telling you why it isn't possible.

Describe the voice. Is it male or female? Is it older or younger than you? Is it familiar? (Sometimes we don't like to pin it on one person, so it can be an amalgamation of people – in which case you can create a character.)

What does the voice's owner look like, including, stance, gait, and clothing?
What's their profession?

What are their habits around you and habits when alone?

What does the voice's owner care about and value most?

What are their hobbies or pastimes?

Now give the voice a name. When this saboteur next shows up,
use this check-in question: 'How is it serving me right now to listen
to this voice?' If it isn't, send it off using one of the following methods: send it to
do its favourite hobby/put it in a box/slap a thigh/tell it to go away.

The career saboteur

The majority of clients I've seen over the past decade have come to me because they want a career change. You now know that there's a lot more to it than that, but this is what has brought them to coaching, and what they present as being the issue.

This is because your main self-sabotaging voice will have had a lot to do with your career choice. For example, my dad, after 22 years' service in the army, went and worked for the local council for the next 25 years, until he retired. I recently discovered that his dad had also worked for the local council, and his mum had worked for the tax office. So I come from a line of civil servants. Consequently, my dad firmly believed in a job for life, and all the stability and security that provided, and of course he wanted the same for me. However, the rebel in me felt sick at the thought of working either for the local council or joining the army. Luckily, in spite of his firmly held beliefs, my dad allowed me the option to follow my comparatively unconventional dream of working in television.

However, many of the clients I've seen over the years have not been so fortunate. I have lost count of the number of lawyers, accountants and doctors who have followed their parents' path.

This is particularly important today, as the types of jobs available and ways of working are undergoing a revolution that affects both us and the generations to come. Our parents were born in an age when there were 'jobs for life': they worked for the majority of their adult lives for one employer and retired with a healthy pension. Across the board, even in the public sector, there are now fewer and fewer permanent or secure jobs available. Our parents' views, beliefs and the advice they give generally do not apply in today's workplace.

This becomes even more important when we think about advising our own children on their choice of career – again based on our experiences, beliefs and desire to keep them safe in life. Just this week I have had to be extremely careful when supporting my daughter in choosing her GCSEs. I loved art, and think it would be a great advantage to her to do business studies and computer science. However, she would hate doing those subjects, she isn't me, and already I can see she enjoys different subjects – she chose textiles and food nutrition. Added to this, there is the issue that what I/we know or experience today, in terms of the workplace, will be irrelevant when she and her classmates leave school in just five years' time.

The effects on you

The effects of building and staying in a career that was really chosen by your saboteur can be many. Commonly, you dread getting up and going to work in the morning; your performance suffers; your work/life balance suffers (as you try to block out the feelings with yet more work); you become less present with your friends and family; you lose your spark and you don't know why.

The way you work

It's also important to know your saboteur can have a major effect on how you work. Many of us have been conditioned to believe that we need to work long hours, with work being a priority and the enjoyment of life secondary, and that we should work all our adult lives only to enjoy ourselves once we retire. This can have a huge impact on us, especially when it comes to work/life balance, stress levels and mental health. This way of working is another common denominator amongst my clients.

One of my recent clients found it increasingly difficult to work less and kept taking on more and more responsibility and adding to his workload whenever he was asked. He was in a senior management role, doing very well, had just been promoted, but was finding it very hard to leave the office and actually stop working. This was leaving him with little or no capacity for his home life, his marriage, seeing friends, let alone include time for any exercise or managing to eat well. This left him frazzled, anxious, exhausted and heading for burnout.

It was only when he identified his father, a hard-working, retired manager in the manufacturing sector, that he realized what hia father had always told him had been sabotaging his own mental health:

01. You need to add value.
02. You need to go above and beyond.
03. You can't let anyone down.
04. You have to give it your all.
05. Now is not the time to stand still.
06. You can rest when you're 65.

This tone of sabotaging voice is one I see frequently in my organizational work. I was recently invited to do a workshop with a group of senior managers in the finance sector – the employer was very progressive in terms of wellbeing, but had noticed that in spite of their push for better work practices, people would still work too hard and spend too long in the office.

'It's not what you say out of your mouth that determines your life, it's what you whisper to yourself that has the most power!'

ROBERT T. KIYOSAKI

In the workshop, I shared the results of a scientific study which stated that once we hit 40 years-plus, we should only be doing 3–5 hours of cognitive-based work (thinking, reasoning, using our memory and judgement) per day – anything beyond this was pushing our brain and body into a state of stress. What came out of the session was that even though the head of department was telling people to work fewer hours, take more breaks and get more sleep, the employees' sabotaging voices were resisting these instructions. It was only when they went off into pairs to identify these voices, and came back to discuss their findings with the group, that people realized how those voices had been preventing them from taking better care of themselves at work – both physically and mentally.

This is not unusual. Remember we have been brought up by parents working in a different age where they were taught that work was not for enjoyment and rest would come after retirement.

Once they had identified those voices, and had been given some tools, techniques and alternatives, they did see there was a different way to work – and one that would actually help them be more, rather than less, productive.

WHAT DID YOUR CAREER SABOTEUR CHOOSE FOR YOU?

What career or type of role did your saboteur choose for you?

Why did that voice believe it was the best route for you?

What was the fear behind that?

Put that voice aside and write down your fantasy job/career/vocation.

YOUR FUTURE SELF – THE VOICE YOU CAN TRUST

You know those articles where they ask celebrities what advice they would give their 20-year-old self? Well this is the equivalent, only you get all of that great advice and wisdom from yourself in the future – right now. 'Future Self' is a great tool and I have been using it with my clients ever since it had a huge impact on me during my training. It's a way of going forward in time and meeting your older, wiser self, who is living a happier, healthier, more fulfilled life, based on having made the best decisions and most positive changes.

In my personal and professional experience, the most effective way to dramatically change the course of the rest of your life, to feel happier and fulfilled, is to get a grip on your main sabotaging voice and start using your Future Self. Studies in clinical psychology, and more recently in positive psychology, also show that when we feel connected to our Future Self we feel more optimistic, and are more likely to make better decisions and choices in the present. They show it helps bolster our willpower and deal with those pesky saboteurs, as we find it easier to say no to anything that gets in the way of our goals and dreams. Our Future Self is a personalized representation of our goals, our most 'cherished self-wishes' as one psychologist has put it so beautifully. It brings clarity to our true priorities in life, our motivations and real values. When we are connected to all of these things, we can gain a sense of purpose, a feeling of greater control over our lives, can improve our performance, and increase our happiness.

Decision-making

For big life decisions, working with our Future Self is extremely useful, as it cuts through our tendency to agonize and stress over something for days, weeks or even months on end. Last year I landed a great corporate coaching job, which would have meant a lot of work and a good income for me over the next two years. I went through the whole interview process, I even went away for a weekend of training. As more details started to emerge, I realized that I would actually have to start spending a lot of time away from my daughter, she would have to go and live with her dad more, and I may even have to hire someone to look after her while I was away – something I had resisted since she was born. I went back and forth with this for a while, but then connected with my Future Self (more

on what this involves later), and she said: 'Amelie will only have one childhood, and when you look back on these years what will you be glad about? It certainly won't be that you were away a lot travelling and working, but it would be that you were there for her during that time. You'll find other work, and you'll be there for her – that's what's most important.'

Suddenly it all felt very clear, and turning down that work was one of the best decisions I've ever made. My dear friend who did go on and work on the project was away so much it would just have been awful for me and Amelie. Of course I did get other work that more than made up for the loss of money. In the moment, without having that wise voice to check in with, I know how scary and confusing these decisions can be.

Fear and anxiety

Your Future Self instantly gives you a way to cut through all of the fear, and the sabotaging voices, enabling you to make the best and wisest decisions – at any given moment.

When that fear (of not doing the right thing, having enough money, missing out on 'amazing' opportunities, etc.) comes along – it can lead to some very short-sighted, poor decision-making. Conversely,

'I am often plagued by self-doubt and anxieties and can find it hard to see a way out of my current set-up. However, since meeting my Future Self, I have found the strength and confidence to carry on fighting and believe that I have options, and it is down to me to make a change. She reminds me that I am a fighter and survivor!'

ANON

making decisions from that wiser, longer-term view, and consequently being more aware of your values, really does lead you to design the life you really want to be living, and means that you will feel happier and more fulfilled in the long run.

Doing the Co-Active Training Institute visualization exercise on the following pages and using this tool myself has had a huge effect on my life. I vividly remember lying on the floor alongside 18 other people who were also training to become coaches (this was a bit of a stretch for me back then – lying down with a load of people I barely knew and doing a visualization which was still a bit hippy-dippy and new to me). I went with it, as I hope you will too. When I came out of that visualization I realized, and it clarified, what I knew deep down: that the path I was on was not the right one for me. It gave me the clarity and the courage to change course.

To meet your Future Self you can ask a trusted friend or supportive person to read out the two-part guided visualizations included on the following pages. You can also go to www.suebelton.com/bookresources for my audio recordings. Whichever method you choose, please do not read it out yourself, as you need to be able to actually do the visualization.

MEET YOUR FUTURE SELF

I recommend you do the first visualization and answer the questions, then allow at least a couple of days before you do the second, which will give you an instant way of connecting with your Future Self in any given moment.

Visualization 1

Get into a comfortable position. Allow your eyes to close and begin by focusing your awareness on your breath, breathing in and breathing out. Breathe in easily and effortlessly, and then breathe out. Each breath allows you to become more relaxed and comfortable. Outside sounds only allow you to go deeper inside: a reminder of how good it is to leave the noise and stress of the outside world and journey into the quiet and peace of your inner world.

As you relax, you will find yourself becoming quieter and more peaceful. Now bring your attention to the spot between your eyes: the third eye. Imagine a light there. What colour is the light between your eyes? Now imagine that light becoming a beam that extends out into space. Follow that beam as it leaves this building, as it travels above the city and continues out, so that you can view the entire area. Keep going further and further into space and notice the curvature of the Earth. As you keep going further and further out, you find yourself enveloped by the softness and quiet of space. Notice the big blue-green ball below you with the white clouds swirling around it. Allow yourself to enjoy this perspective for a moment.

Now notice another beam of light very close to you, a different colour from the one you followed into space. Begin to follow that beam back down to Earth. The beam is taking you back to Earth 20 years from now, 20 years into the future. As you come closer to the end of the beam, keep noticing where you are. This is where your Future Self lives – you, 20 years from now. Come into contact with Earth and notice where you are. Notice what surrounds you. Now move to the dwelling of your Future Self. What does it look like? What kind of landscape does it have? Are there trees or flowers? What kind? Get a sense of this place.

Now have someone come to the door. On the other side of the door is your Future Self, waiting to greet you – it is you, 20 years from now. As the door opens, what do you notice? Greet your Future Self and notice the way your Future Self returns your greeting, welcoming you into this time and place 20 years in the future. Take in this person, your Future Self.

Now move with your Future Self to a comfortable place for a conversation. Perhaps your Future Self offers you something to drink. Settle in and make yourself comfortable for a talk with your Future Self. There are questions that you might want to ask your Future Self. Begin by asking: 'What is it that you most remember about the past 20 years?'

Bringing this visit to a close, thank your Future Self for being here with you today and sharing so much wisdom.

Now find your way back to the beam of light and journey back along the beam, watching this world of 20 years in the future grow ever smaller as you move out into space. Again, you see the blue-green ball below you with clouds swirling around it. Notice that your beam of light has intersected with a different beam of light that will bring you back to the present. Follow this beam of light and as you travel down it, notice the Earth growing bigger and bigger. Moving further down the beam, notice the geography of the area, the skyline and landscape, and, finally, come back into this room. Good. In a few moments, I'm going to count from three down to one. At the count of one, you will be refreshed and alert, as if you've had the perfect amount of rest, knowing you can remember everything you wish of this inner journey.

When you open your eyes, please remain silent and jot down things you want to remember about your journey. Three. Coming back to the present, becoming more alert and refreshed. Two. Stretching your body, feeling the ground beneath you. And one. Eyes open, refreshed and alert.

Post-visualization questions

What did your Future Self look like?

How did they seem/feel?

Where did they live?

What are the colours, sights, sounds, smells of their home?

What is it that you most remember
about the past 20 years?

What do you need to know to get yourself from where you are now to where you are going? What would be most helpful?'

What were the answers to any other questions
you asked?

What name do you want to use for them?

In between visualization questions

Lie or sit somewhere comfortable where you know you won't be interrupted.
Revisit your Future Self as best you can, and ask them the following questions:

How do they spend their spare time?

Who and what do they most love in their life?

Do they have a favourite painting/song? (If so put the painting up/
play the song every morning.)

Visualization 2

Make yourself comfortable and allow your eyes to close. Begin by taking long, slow, deep breaths. Breathe in through your nose and hold it ... then breathe out through your mouth. Just allow yourself to be aware of your breathing: easily, naturally and freely.

I'm now going to invite you to take a mental inventory of your body. Beginning at the top of your head, become aware of any tension or tightness you might find. Give that tension or tightness a colour and let it drain out from the tips of your toes and the tips of your fingers; just allow that tension or tightness to drain away. Moving down your body, bring your attention to your neck and arms. Again, if you find any tension or tightness, just let it drain away. Now take your awareness down along your back, into your abdomen and pelvic area. Again, notice any tightness you might find there and eliminate it. Imagine ii melting away, draining out through the tips of your toes. Notice if there is any tension or tightness in your legs, ankles and feet and just allow it to drain out through your toes. Now imagine you're like a strong and sturdy tree, putting roots down into the ground, allowing those roots to go deeper and deeper, spreading out, connecting you to the Earth.

Now bring your attention to the spot between your eyes: the third eye. Imagine a light there. What colour is the light between your eyes? Now imagine that light becoming a beam that extends out into space. Follow that beam as it leaves this building, as it travels above the city and continues out, so that you can view the entire area. Keep going further and further into space and notice the curvature of the Earth. As you keep going further and further out, you find yourself enveloped by the softness and quiet of space. Notice the big blue-green ball below you with the white clouds swirling around it. Allow yourself to enjoy this perspective for a moment.

Now notice another beam of light very close to you – a different colour to the one you followed into space. Begin to follow that beam back down to Earth. The beam is taking you back to Earth 20 years from now, 20 years into the future. Keep following this beam down.

As you come closer to the end of the beam, keep noticing where you are. This is where your Future Self lives – you, 20 years from now. Come into contact with Earth and notice where you are. Now go to the dwelling of your Future Self. You know the way. You've been here before. Your Future Self is waiting for you. Waiting to talk with you. As your Future Self greets you, notice what it is like being with this person again. Look around you. Soak up the environment. Notice the colours here.

Now is your opportunity to ask whatever questions you'd like of your Future Self. You might want to know your next step. Who you need to be right now in order to move forwards. Or ask your Future Self anything that feels right to you. (Pause) Now take a moment to listen to your Future Self's response. (Long pause)

I am now going to invite you to take a deep breath and allow yourself to step into the being of your Future Self. Allow yourself to merge into this person's body. Experience what it feels like to be this Future Self. Be aware of how you feel. Of how good it feels in your Future Self's body. What does the world look like through your Future Self's eyes? Walk around, feeling yourself move as your Future Self. Notice if there's one particular place in your body where you can feel your Future Self's power most strongly. This is the power of being your Future Self. Allow that feeling to expand, filling your whole body, entering your cells. You may want to touch that place on your body in order to anchor this feeling. Know that whenever you wish to connect with your Future Self, you can touch that place on your body and bring out these positive, powerful feelings. When you touch that place, these feelings and this experience will flood your body, easily and effortlessly.

Now, looking out through your Future Self's eyes, look at your Present-day Self. What do you notice about your Present-day Self? Looking out through your Future Self's eyes, what is it that you want to tell your Present-day Self? (Pause)

Now take a deep breath and shift your awareness, leaving the body of your Future Self and becoming your Present-day Self once again. Allow yourself to be fully present in the body of your Present-day Self.

As you look back at your Future Self, notice that this person has a gift for you: something to remind you of who you are becoming and what you are moving towards. As your Future Self offers you the gift, ask if there's any meaning to it. Is there anything you need to know about it? (Pause)

It's time to leave now. Thank your Future Self for the wisdom.
From now on, your Future Self will be an inner resource you can use whenever you need to do so. Whenever you seek guidance, whenever you need to know what your next step should be, you can contact your Future Self. Say good-bye, knowing that you will remember everything you need to from this visit.

Now find your way back to the beam of light and journey back along the beam, watching this world of 20 years in the future grow ever smaller as you move out into space. Again, you see the blue-green ball below you with clouds swirling around it. Notice that your beam of light has intersected with a different beam of light that will bring you back to the present. Follow this beam of light and as you travel down it, notice the Earth growing bigger and bigger. Moving further down the beam, notice the geography of the area, the skyline and landscape, and, finally, come back into this room.

In a few moments, I'm going to count from three down to one. At the count of one, you will be refreshed and alert, as if you've had the perfect amount of rest, knowing you can remember everything you wish of this inner journey.

Three. Coming back now, coming back to present time, becoming more alert and refreshed. Two. Stretching your body, feeling the ground beneath you. And one. Eyes open, refreshed and alert.

Post-visualization questions

What's your next step?

Who do you need to be right now in order to move forwards?

Write down the answers to any other questions you asked your Future Self.

Looking through their eyes, what did you want to tell yourself?

What was the place in your body you felt her/his presence most strongly?

What was the gift?

Did it have any meaning?

Ways to start using your Future Self

Next time you have an internal dilemma, ask yourself,
'What would my Future Self do?'
Connect with them and note down what they say.

Before going to an important meeting or event, connect with your
Future Self and go in as them. How did this feel?

The next time someone asks you to do something you don't really want to do but
feel torn, consult your Future Self – what do they think?

The next time you are involved in a conflict with someone, or have to deal with a person who always antagonizes you, ask your Future Self how to handle it. Follow the advice and notice what happens. Note down the result.

Ask your Future Self what work they would be doing. Note it down below.

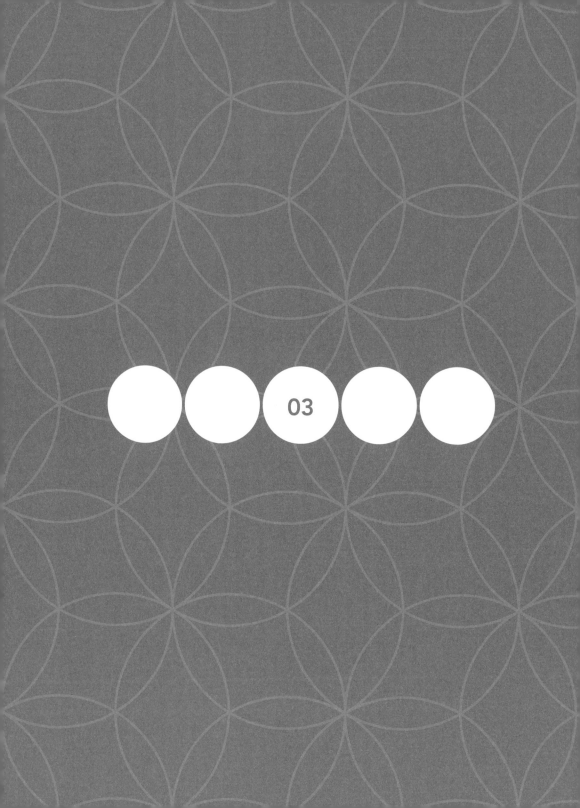

CHOOSE

To pick out the best of two or more alternatives,
to decide on a course of action.

How would it feel to know that whatever life throws at you, rather than feeling powerless, you can choose how you think, feel and respond? What would you do if you could instantly feel more confident in any given situation? How would you feel if you knew you could shift any negative emotions in your body – and replace them with more positive ones?

This chapter and third core principle will help you to find out and take action. You will discover how to open up your mind and try new, more positive ways of thinking and acting. You will also learn how to use your body to feel instantly more confident and shift how you behave.

Finally, you will uncover the negative emotions holding you back, and learn a technique that will loosen their grip on you, allowing you to move forwards and take positive action.

FEELING STUCK? YOU ALWAYS HAVE A CHOICE

The knowledge that in any given moment we all actually have a choice was the first major realization I gained through my own experience of coaching. Up until that time, possibly like you, I felt that I was at the mercy of certain things in my life.

I really thought that there were many circumstances that I was powerless over or had no choice about: a mortgage to pay; a young child to support; an unhappy relationship; the fact that I was suffering from anxiety and on medication; that I lived somewhere I hated; that I had been working in television and radio for my entire adult life and didn't know how to do anything else, let alone run my own business. In addition to these circumstances, I held some pretty rigid opinions and beliefs about 'how things go' and 'that's just the way it is'. Yes, these things may be fixed, but what isn't fixed is how you view them, and what you think and feel about them – all of which you *can* change.

Choice Theory was developed by Dr William Glasser in the USA in the 1950s and '60s, and is used by thousands of therapists around the world to treat patients for addiction, anxiety and. depression. His model states that every part of our behaviour – our thoughts, feelings, physiology, is a choice. Every single part of it. Although feelings and physical responses are harder to control, we *do* have a choice when it comes to our thoughts and actions, which have an impact on the other responses. Glasser argues that we have full control over our 'total behaviour', and when we live a life based on choice, we are more responsible and more empowered. His

theory is that nobody can 'make' us do or feel anything, all we do is give or receive information from others, and it is our choice as to how we perceive, process and respond.

As Glasser says: 'The only person I can really control is myself. If I think others can control me, and so are to blame for all that goes on in my life, I tend to do nothing effective and head for frustration. This is not to deny that we can be subjected to violent and coercive situations, but while we are alive we have choices even in these situations. In the worst situations these choices may not be enough to save us or they may be painful or they may be choices we wish we never had to make. For instance a person in an abusive situation may have to choose whether to stay or go, though both choices are painful – there is, nevertheless, a choice and that realization may empower the person to choose to get away.' I agree 100 per cent.

Change your mind and your life

Glasser's therapy model focuses on changing our behaviours in order to change our lives, but I'm going to ask you to go one step further and change what you think and believe, and then after that, change your behaviours to match your new way of being.

During the course of my first ever coaching session, which took place over the

> 'Choice is the most powerful tool we have. Everything boils down to choice. We exist in a field of infinite possibilities. Every choice we make shuts an infinite number of doors and opens an infinite number of doors. At any point, we can change the direction of our lives by a simple choice. It's all in our hands, our hearts and our minds.'
>
> TINYBUDDHA.COM

phone, my coach took me from the depths of fear and despair to a place of hope and possibility, where I no longer felt a victim of circumstance. From there I was able to start taking back control of my life. It was an incredible, life-changing experience, and one which ultimately led me to where I am now.

If you think about any set of circumstances, you do have a choice as to how you are going to think and feel about them. Imagine being diagnosed with terminal cancer. You can choose to say to yourself, 'This is not happening, I'm going to fight this, I'll live.' While at the other end of the scale you can say, 'I am going to die and I accept this, and I am going to enjoy my last days with my family, and this is okay.'

This is when you realize there is a choice. You may not be able to change the situation (in most cases), but you can certainly change how you think and feel about it and then how you respond to it.

After my own revelation and mind-blowing experience of doing this, I then went on to learn how to do this with my clients and the following exercise is my version of the Co-Active Training Institute's Formula for Balance Coaching.

THE CHOICE ROOM

Find yourself a private room or space – somewhere you won't be disturbed. Think about one thing in your life you're not happy with, but which you feel 'stuck' with. Place the issue – be it your career or your relationship – in the middle of the room, separating the issue from your perspective (what you think and feel about it now).

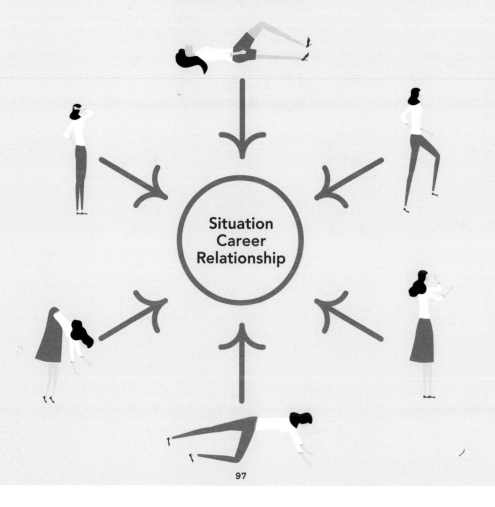

**Situation
Career
Relationship**

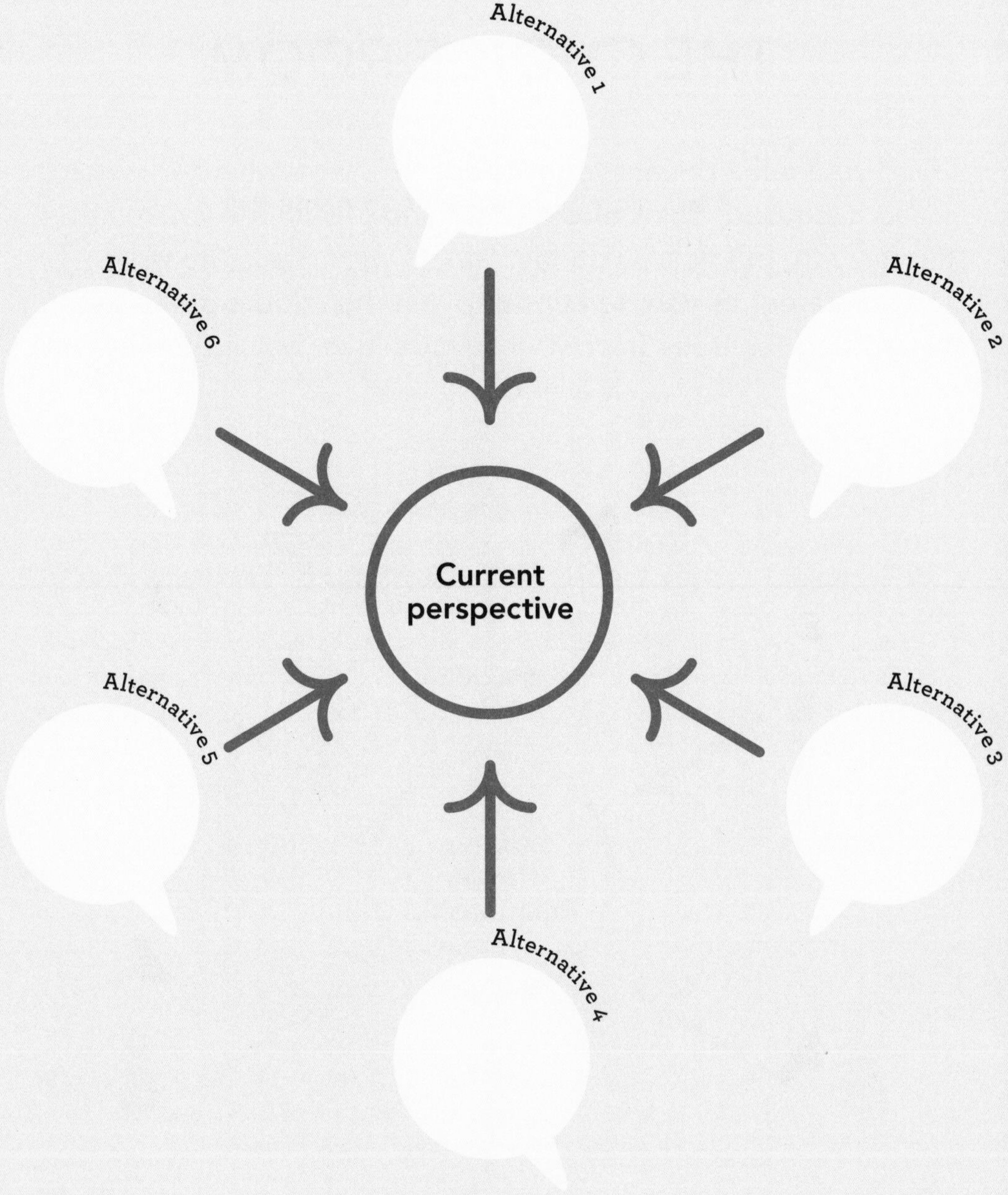
Alternative 1
Alternative 2
Alternative 3
Alternative 4
Alternative 5
Alternative 6
Current perspective

Choose a perspective and name it

From where you are in the room, admit your current perspective (e.g. My job is dead-end and I'll die of boredom if I stay, I feel sad, down etc.) and realize how far you have convinced yourself of this. Go there, embody it, even give it a metaphor or a name.

Try other perspectives

Now that you have clearly defined your current view, this is the fun bit. Try some different ways of thinking and feeling about the issue. Move around the room, using any props within your space. Try lying down on the floor. Some people like to take on a character or an emotion as they move. For each new place or body position (try five or six), take time to notice what you think, believe, feel and would be doing about your issue. Try naming each perspective, such as 'on the beach' or 'from a window'. Write your new perspectives in the circles opposite.

Choose

When you feel you have enough perspectives, revisit each one – either mentally or literally. Do you want to stay in that first one? No? Then move around and choose the one you most want to go with right now. Maybe you tried lying down on your sofa, and that reminded you of lying on the beach, and here you really feel that whatever the situation, anything is achievable. Imagine all of the things you would be believing and doing from this new place. Write down the name of this perspetive.

Create a manifesto

In your new perspective, now create a manifesto (like the one opposite) describing how you are going to be, and what you are going to do about the issue at hand. Write it out and refer back to it as much as possible. Give your manisfesto a name, for example, The Beach Manifesto.

SAMPLE MANIFESTO

- I will accept how things are at the moment and vow to take regular daily action towards my new chosen career (whatever that is).

- I will sleep seven hours a night to help me stay on track with this (with one-hour of no TV/screens before bed).

- I will spend 30 minutes each morning researching the roles available in the field I'd love to work in.

- I will connect with one person a week in this field.

- I will switch off my FB/Insta alerts and only check my feeds once a day.

- I will take a proper lunch break of 30 minutes and go and eat my lunch away from my desk – outside if not raining.

- I will stop complaining about my work.

- I will be more grateful for all that I do have in my life already.

Create an anchor

You may want to create an anchor or structure to help connect you back to your new perspective – especially if you feel yourself slipping back to the old one. This can be an image of a beautiful beach, a rock or an item of clothing.

Note down what this anchor is.

EMBODIMENT

It is not just our mindset and what we do that we can change: how we choose to move our bodies has a direct impact on the way we think, feel and behave. I touched on this briefly in the Choice Room exercise, but now I want to examine it further.

Numerous neuroscientific studies and the results of research into the mind-body connection show that much of our behaviour is embodied (i.e. held in the body). For example, smiling makes you feel happier; sitting on a hard surface makes you negotiate harder; standing up straight makes you more confident (and less likely to be bullied); slouching makes you feel sad.

In her inspiring TED Talk 'Your body language shapes who you are', social scientist Amy Cuddy shares her research. She states that by standing in a 'power pose' we can make ourselves *feel* more powerful, behave more powerfully, and change certain outcomes in our life. She conducted a study at Harvard University, where participants sat in either a high-power pose (expansive posture) or low-power pose (leaning inwards, with legs crossed) for two minutes. She found that those who sat in the high-power pose felt more powerful and performed better in mock interviews than those who had not. She also claims that power posing actually changes body chemistry – increasing levels of testosterone (said to be good for confidence and assertiveness) and decreasing levels of cortisol (the stress hormone). This is vital, she says, for powerful and effective leadership and I would argue any situation where you want to feel more confident and less stressed. She also says there is a gender difference, possibly due to women's lower levels of testosterone. Like me, she's also an advocate of the 'fake it till you make it method'.

HARNESS YOUR WONDER WOMAN

- Think of a situation in which you would like to feel more confident.
- Decide and name how you want to feel and behave, e.g. solid/confident/sure. If there's someone who does this well, name them.
- Stand up. Put your hands on your hips or up above your head as if you've just crossed the finishing line of a race. Plant your feet firmly on the ground, with your legs hip distance apart.
- Take some long, deep breaths and imagine the feeling in your body.
- Imagine what you would be doing, saying, thinking and feeling from this place.
- Walk around. Notice how you move, walk 'into' this feeling.
- Embody this way of being.
- Once you have it think of an 'anchor' that will remind you of it – a piece of clothing, jewellery, shoes.
- The next time you go into the relevant situation repeat these actions beforehand, and as much as possible, throughout the encounter.

YOUR EMOTIONS

Because difficult emotions can be so unpleasant we often try and rid ourselves of them as quickly as possible (I know I did). But we can choose to change our emotions – even the difficult ones. If you do this, you will dramatically change your life.

These difficult or 'negative' emotions are the ones we all experience at one time or another, and they fall under three main categories:

- Anger (rage, frustration, disappointment, resentment).

- Fear (anxiety, hesitation, doubt, lack of trust in self and others).

- Sadness (helplessness, victim mentality, apathy, indifference).

Avoiding, suppressing or controlling these difficult emotions takes a great deal of mental and physical energy. More importantly, it also prevents us from moving forwards in our lives, seeing what we can learn from them, and living our best life. Have a look at the list opposite – which of these is your most common 'go-to' emotion? Mine is fear and anxiety, and until I experienced CTI's *Process coaching method* (a method of taking a client *into* these emotions instead of avoiding them), they dominated my life. I often woke up anxious – about the day ahead, what needed to be done, the future, where I would live, what I would do with my career, etc. You can easily see how, when I was constantly feeling like this (and trying so hard *not* to), I wasn't going to be getting much else done – let alone look at what I might be able to do in the future. By processing these emotions (going to them, allowing them to flow through my body, being *with* them), they no longer control me – most of the time.

Emotions as information

In his book *Magnificent Addiction*, Philip Kavanaugh Ph.D., says that it is our need to *control* these negative emotions that is at the root of all addiction. Indeed, he says that it is often the control of negative emotions that is the 'master addiction'. The theory is that often, from a young age, we are taught *not* to be with these emotions: *not* to feel angry, *not* to feel upset. How many times have you heard people say, 'Don't cry'? We may even have been rewarded with a sweet treat to stop us feeling upset or hurt (now there's an obvious link to comfort eating). Feeling these negative emotions often becomes seen as bad – and shame is then added on top of the emotion itself. Most of the time, the intention of those around us and their response to us is not malicious – they just don't want us to feel sad, or simply can't be with those emotions themselves. The irony is that if we were allowed to feel the emotion, it would pass relatively quickly. It's said that any emotion takes approximately 20–30 seconds to run its course through our body. You can see it when a young child is allowed to cry they bounce back very quickly. By robbing ourselves of having this full experience – of feeling and experiencing everything, good or bad – we are robbing ourselves of having the best life possible in its fullest range.

We are also denying ourselves the information that these emotions provide. There is a theory in neuroscience known as the Embodied Brain, which holds that we have a whole nervous system in our gut (commonly referred to as our intuition), a neural system in our heart (referred to as having feelings in our heart), and that all of the information and emotions from those neural systems feeds into our brain via the vagus nerve. By ignoring all of our (often physical) negative emotions, feelings and sensations, we are thus ignoring a wealth of vital information, and narrowing our learning and experience of life.

The link to illness

When this happens, we are both denying ourselves the information being sent via these emotions, and denying our bodies the natural physiological process of release. How many times have you experienced this, – just by allowing yourself to have a good cry – don't you always feel just that little bit better and more optimistic after? If we do not allow our bodies to do this, to discharge these feelings freely, these blocked emotions will drain our mental energy, and can even lead to serious health problems.

Numerous studies have shown that negative feelings and attitudes can create

'It's the hiding, denying, submerging that gets clients into trouble ... when they do go in, they discover more about themselves, become more resourceful, and release energy in the emotion – what we refer to as e-motion – to motivate new movement.'

HENRY KIMSEY-HOUSE, KAREN KIMSEY-HOUSE, PHILIP SANDAHL AND LAURA WHITWORTH

stress, which depletes the brain chemicals required for happiness, and damages the immune system. Stress has also been shown to reduce our life span, affecting our DNA strands and causing us to age more quickly. Poorly managed or repressed anger has also been linked to several conditions, such as high blood pressure, cardiovascular disease and digestive disorders. High levels of cynicism in later life have been linked to both a greater risk of dementia and heart disease, as well as earlier death in women. Hostility (being antagonistic, bitter, unkind and angry towards others), has been linked with a higher risk of stroke. Then there's depression, which has been linked to an increased risk for Type 2 diabetes, heart attack, and disability in later life. That's quite a list.

One theory is that when you're stressed or depressed, cortisol levels increase, making your immune system less able to control inflammation in the body, which may lead to disease over time. I would also argue that when you feel low, you are more likely to smoke or drink, and less likely to exercise or take good care of yourself, and this in turn has a negative impact on your brain and body.

Louise Hay, world-renowned teacher and lecturer on self-healing, goes one stage further. In her best-selling books *Heal Your Body* and *You Can Heal Your Life*, she lists and directly links, specific negative emotions and thoughts with physical ailments. After being diagnosed with 'incurable' cervical cancer in the 1970s, she concluded that holding on to resentment about her childhood abuse and rape had contributed to its onset. She reported how she refused conventional medical treatment, and cured her cancer with a regime of forgiveness, therapy, nutrition, reflexology and colonic enemas. This has certainly struck a chord with many, as have her recommendations to replace negative thoughts with new, positive affirmations.

Whatever your thoughts about this, don't you think it might be a good idea to experience a few seconds of unpleasantness for the sake of a whole lot of learning and a richer, healthier life? If not, let me put it this way: if you don't want to feel bad, where you 'can't go' is exactly where you need to go.

If you don't want to be plagued by worry – go there. If you can no longer stand the disappointment you feel about how your life has turned out – go there. If you hate feeling so angry all of the time – go there. If you're scared of risk and about taking the next step – go there. If you don't, you will spend so much time and energy trying to avoid these feelings that your life will be dominated by denial and avoidance.

Your life will also become limited. You are much more likely to behave in destructive ways, and to use various avoidance or 'sticking-plaster' techniques, which give a temporarily sense of relief

and suppress those negative emotions. Drinking, working excessive hours, drug-taking, 'comfort' eating, social media addiction, sex, shopping. All of these things give us a temporary hit of the feel-good hormone dopamine, but the problem is that you have to keep doing them more and more, and the emotion you are trying to distract yourself from will still keep coming back.

What kind of life do you want to live? One full of negative emotions and denial, plus any number of destructive, life-numbing avoidance behaviours? Or do you choose to live *with* these emotions, allowing them to work their way through your body and dissipate, and discovering and learning what they are trying to teach you? If you're ready for the latter, look at the three-part process on the following pages, which explain how to deal with and shift negative emotions.

SIT WITH IT

I am going to invite you to do something completely counter-intuitive. Instead of avoiding a negative emotion and trying to get rid of it as quickly as possible, I am going to ask you to do the exact opposite – sit with it. Find a comfortable, quiet space where you won't be interrupted.

Accept

Go to a difficult emotion you feel about something that's happening in your life. As soon as you are aware of this emotion, take a moment and accept it; you can even state (internally or externally) 'I feel angry' or 'I feel sad'. The key here is not to try and escape from it or push it away – this is what often happens, and that is why the pause is helpful here. Identify the emotion and write it down.

Allow

Once you have taken the big steps of accepting and identifying the emotion, next (and this is usually the frightening bit we don't do) let it run through your body. Allow yourself to feel it. Go to where it is in your body – and although it will feel scary, know that nothing bad is actually going to happen to you. You may experience the emotion as a tight feeling in your chest, an ache in your stomach, a constriction in your throat, but however you do, really let yourself go there, give it your full attention. Notice it and be curious: what colour is it? What is its texture? Is it moving? Is it solid or made up of many different particles?

Once you have done this, breathe down into it, and allow the breath to fill it up with new, fresh air. Notice what happens to it: what happens to the shape, the texture, its density? While you are doing this, your brain will try and pull you away – this is all normal, but just keep coming back to where you are consciously focusing your attention.

It is the act of going there and staying there (versus avoidance or suppression) that is important. Courage and patience is required – but it is worth it, I promise you. When you have done this successfully, you will ultimately feel that shift, that dissipation, that sense of calm.

Ask

What is this emotion telling me? What is the message?

What's possible from here?

What is the one thing I need to accept about this situation?

What is one thing I can do about this situation?

All emotions are messages from the body. The next time you receive one of these messages, I ask that you try this process, and in doing so choose another way to feel and be.

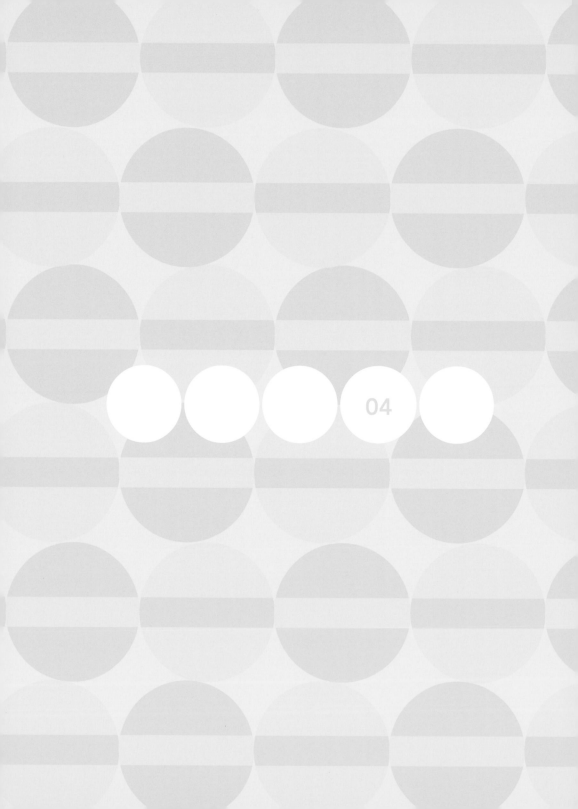

04

CELEBRATE

From the Latin *celebrare* meaning 'to honour'; to acknowledge a significant event, honour or praise publicly.

Do you constantly re-examine past mistakes or compare yourself to others (especially via social media) and conclude that you fall short? Do you feel like a fraud and worry that you are about to be found out? Does your perfectionism cause you to procrastinate or work yourself harder and harder to get things 'perfect'?

This chapter is about discovering why we are so hard on ourselves, how this holds us back in our lives, and what to do about it. You will discover the source of these thoughts and behaviours, and learn not to berate yourself for past mistakes or compare yourself to others. You will develop the awareness and the tools to combat imposter syndrome or perfectionism. You will come to see the benefits of self-acknowledgement and self-compassion, and the importance of celebrating who you are, what you bring, and what you have already achieved.

I'M NOT GOOD ENOUGH

This is the most common underlying fear among my clients, and it's the biggest and most difficult to overcome. Gone unchallenged, this belief will seriously limit the extent to which you truly live your life, and will hold you back from achieving your goals and dreams.

The feeling that you're not good enough is one that affects everyone, although it shows up differently in different people. It can manifest itself as over-achievement and an attempt to prove that you are worthy or accomplished; it can cause you constantly to make comparisons; it can also lead to perfectionism, procrastination, avoidance or an inability to complete tasks or projects. Unfortunately, it can be possible for people to experience all of the above – depending on the time and situation.

Where does it come from?

Buried inside you are hidden beliefs that are currently running your life – beliefs about the world, about other people and yourself. These are formed during childhood, and as a result are extremely simplistic; yet they have the power to dictate many of your daily decisions. As discussed in Conquer, when you are a child the most influential adults are usually your parents, followed closely by other relatives and teachers. Whatever you are told you take on as being the truth. When I hear debilitating beliefs from my clients, I look at the root causes and over the years I have identified four main types of saboteurs that lead to feelings of not being good enough:

The pushy parent will tell their children to 'work harder'; 'there are only winners and losers'; 'you need to be top of the class'. This is most common one I see, and it generally leads to over-achieving, stress and burnout. It stems from the deep belief that you are only ever worthy when you are achieving. There is also little acknowledgement or joy in the wins along the way and a need to always do more.

The nervous over-protector uses phrases such as 'be careful, people might not like that'; 'do you think that's really possible for you'; 'what if you can't do it?' Commonly coming from mothers, this one leads to doubt and fear, and settling for the safer option.

The comparer will say 'your brother's the academic one'; 'why can't you get an A like Alice'. Always falling short, you will constantly compare yourself to others.

The labeller uses phrases such as 'you're lazy'; 'you're naughty'; 'you're too unfocused'. A classic style of parenting passed down through the ages, people honestly believed this helps children to correct their behaviour and achieve more in life. On the contrary, this leads to a deep level of shame – that you feel inherently bad or wrong at your core.

All of these parenting styles basically leave you believing you are not good enough as you are right now – enough meaning deserving, worthy of love and mattering to others. Unchecked, this fear could have you

spending your whole life either not bothering to try things or trying so hard to prove you are good enough, and never feeling satisfied or enjoying life.

Easy as it is to label these sources, it's important to note that most parents, even if they fall into these somewhat simplistic categories, didn't actually intend to make you feel bad about yourself – they genuinely thought (again because of how they were raised), that this was the right way of helping you have the best life possible.

When you are a child, the most important thing to you is gaining the love and affection of your primary caregivers – usually your parents. However, if your parents are unable or unwilling to give you the love and affection you need, want and deserve, you do not have the capacity at that time to understand that this is their problem and is nothing to do with you. In fact, what happens is often quite the opposite – you think 'it must be me', you try to resolve the situation, and when this does not happen you feel it is your fault – that you are not good enough. This is a heavy burden to carry.

Those with family experiences of alcoholism, depression and domestic violence often form unconscious beliefs from an early age such as, 'If only I behaved better, this wouldn't be happening'; 'If I do really

well in school and get a good report maybe my parents won't fight'.

As children we learn early on that if our parents are happy, they are much more able to give and express the love we need from them. Children cannot fix their parents' problems, so the negative message of 'I couldn't fix it, so I am not good enough,' tends to stick.

Comparison is crippling

It is not only as a child that we need to feel loved, accepted and to belong. In order to survive as an adult, we also need this from the society and culture that we are part of. Like our families, there are many ideas and expectations in today's world that we are expected to live up to – whether we like it or not. In order to be accepted we can't help but compare ourselves to others who appear to be achieving, those who are 'successful', and those who have the 'ideal' life.

Thanks to social media we are forced not only to compare ourselves to the people around us, we are now party to the lives of billions of others. This is an important point.

Think about it: what you are focusing on, and comparing your whole self and 'worthiness' to, is someone's carefully selected highlight of a chosen aspect of their life. You will never see the anxiety, fear, tears, failure and all-round human condition of this person.

Just recently, I was on a business accelerator course and had the misfortune to fall into this comparison trap. I literally got to the point of freaking out every time I read one of the #wins posts – posted by other people on the course celebrating their achievements. It filled me with complete anxiety, fear, terror even. It was crippling. It was only when I went away for the new year to a remote part of the country that had very limited internet connection that I started to feel better about myself. I turned off all my social media notifications to stop them flooding in when connection was restored. I immediately started feeling better able to acknowledge what I was doing in my business, what I was achieving and the lovely clients I was already working with. When I came back after that holiday, I noticed such a difference that I decided to keep those notifications turned off – something I have maintained to this day. In doing so, I was able to go at my pace but most importantly, I was much better able to acknowledge my own achievements.

Instant gratification

We live in an age when we can receive an instant hit of the feel-good hormone dopamine, as well as a simultaneous boost to our self-worth, simply by someone 'liking' our post or 'following' us. The problem is that this becomes a literal measure of our self-worth – and there is always someone who has more likes or more followers. What happens when you don't get as many likes the next time you post? An instant feeling of despondency. On top of that, if we try and do something or achieve something that doesn't give us an instant result, once again this makes us feel that we are 'not good enough'. Not only does this have an immediate impact on our self-worth, focus and motivation, it also leaves us with an increased lack of patience to work at things and to appreciate that things take time to achieve. It has been widely noted that this is extremely worrying for the next generations of children, who are growing up with social media.

So you can see how all of this – our family history, the expectations of our wider culture, and the global 'standards' we are exposed to on an hourly basis – can lead to us feeling 'not good enough', and unable to see that it is possible to make a change, because why should we bother when we will never be as good as 'them'?

COMPARISON DETOX

Find a quiet space where you won't be interrupted. Think about how much time you spend on social media and how this makes you feel. Answer the questions below.

List the ways in which you don't feel good enough. For example: my body is not good enough; I don't do enough; I'm not motivated enough. Allocate these beliefs a score on a scale of 1 to 10 with 1 being the least satisfied and 10 being more satisfied.

Turn off your social media notifications. Check social media just once a day.

List the people and social media threads you follow most frequently. Identify which ones make you feel the least positive about yourself. Unfollow them.

After one week rescore your old beliefs about yourself – what do you think and how do you feel about them now?

IMPOSTER SYNDROME

Another way in which I see *'not good enough'* showing up is when clients feel as if they are about to be found out – for not *being* 'good enough'. They feel they don't really 'belong', that they are a 'fraud', or that they don't actually deserve the role they have, their accomplishments, or the recognition they've received.

Even the fabulous Meryl Streep, who has been nominated for more Academy Awards than any other actor (how much more evidence of being 'good enough' can there be?), has experienced this.

Imposter syndrome, a psychological term rather than an actual disorder, refers to a way of thinking and behaving in which people really believe they have only succeeded due to luck, and not because of any talent or actual achievements. This belief is coupled with a real fear of being exposed as a 'fraud'. The 'syndrome' was first named by clinical psychologists Pauline Clance and Suzanne Imes back in 1978, when they hypothesized that this was something high-achieving women experienced. Despite having plenty of

tangible evidence to the contrary, these women remained convinced that they did not deserve their success. Rather, they called their success 'luck' or 'good timing', and dismissed any acknowledgement of their intelligence or competence. Since this initial study, the syndrome has been found to impact both men and women, but, in the latest study on imposter syndrome in 2018, it was still found to be more prevalent in women.

The gender difference

Writing this section has thrown up many unexpected feelings for me. Reading all of the research and study results, questioning whether there is a gender difference (there is always research to prove it either

'You think, "Why would anyone want to see me again in a movie?" And I don't know how to act anyway so why am I doing this?'

MERYL STREEP

way), I don't think I've wanted to face the reality before now. Yes, I've always said to (primarily female) clients, 'there is said to be a gender difference'. Beyond that, I have never really thought about what it has meant for me personally and professionally. I thought I'd done pretty well in my professional life – that I had not really been held back by being a woman, I had always done what I wanted, I had achieved a lot … But I don't think, until now, that I've wanted to face the fact that I could have been limited by the fact I am a woman. Writing this book has forced me to look back, and, when I do, all sorts of memories have come to mind – how I only took a postgraduate degree in journalism *to be taken seriously;* my ever-present fear of public speaking; my deep-seated but hugely powerful feeling that, *as a girl,* I did not and should not have *an opinion on a matte*r. I've no idea

where that latter belief came from, or who might have said it to me. It is in this way that I see imposter syndrome taking hold of, and limiting, so many of the smart and wonderful women I work with.

There is definitely a difference in upbringing from our male contemporaries: as girls we are more likely to be told or believe *'no one likes a show-off'*, or how we should be *'nice, good, modest and lady-like'.* The sad fact is that people do seem to dislike women who acknowledge their own achievements more than men who do the same. I was really shocked when I read about a case in Sheryl Sandberg's book *Lean In.* She cites an experiment in which business students were given a case study to read – that of a successful Silicon Valley venture capitalist. Half of those who look part received a case study featuring the name Heidi Roizen; while for the other half

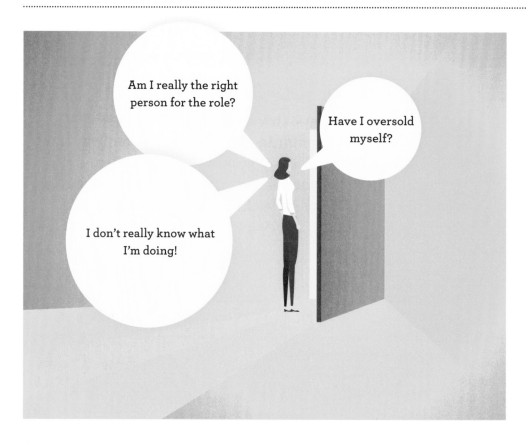

the name 'Heidi' was changed to 'Howard'. The students rated 'Howard' and 'Heidi' as equally competent. However, they liked Howard, but *not* Heidi – viewing her as more 'selfish' and less worthy of being hired. This was exactly the same profile. Remembering our basic human need to belong, it's no wonder that women worry about putting themselves out there and of being proud of their achievements, or of wanting to succeed – when power and success for women is seen as negative.

Until now, there was a part of me that didn't want to admit this: I wanted to believe that we are all regarded and treated as equals. When I scan back over the last decade, I can name woman after woman who has brought this issue to coaching – together with a lack of self-belief – despite evidence to the contrary. Conversely, not one of my male clients has brought this an an all-encompassing issue to coaching.

Added to this, research shows that women and girls are typically more likely to

'The beauty of the impostor syndrome is you vacillate between extreme egomania and a complete feeling of: "I'm a fraud! Oh God, they're on to me! I'm a fraud!" So you just try to ride the egomania when it comes and enjoy it, and then slide through the idea of fraud.'

TINA FEY

internalize failure, mistakes and criticism, while boys and men are more likely to externalize them. The impact of this is that if women don't do well or 'fail', we often see it as yet further evidence that we're not good enough for the role or task at hand – that we are a fraud.

Underrepresentation is a further issue which can trigger impostor feelings. This is because as we all feel more confident in situations where we look like everyone else, and being 'different' can fuel the sense of being a fraud. You can see that if you're the only woman in the boardroom it's going to have an effect.

Imposter syndrome, like comparison, can be utterly debilitating. It can lead to feeling like a failure unless you do more and more training or earn more and more qualifications; to not applying for jobs unless you meet the *exact* criteria; to not asking questions or speaking up in meetings for fear of looking stupid; to not asking for help for fear of looking like a failure; and to pushing yourself harder and harder to *prove* you are good enough. All of these manifestations have a huge impact in themselves and can also cause stress, anxiety, low self-esteem, increased levels of shame, and even depression. Ultimately, imposter syndrome stops you going out in the world, being courageous, seizing opportunities, and living the most meaningful, satisfying life possible.

The key element of imposter syndrome is the ability to internalize your own wins and achievements instead of attributing them to either luck or the work of others. Shifting this mindset is not easy and the exercises on the following pages are intended to help you start doing that.

IMPOSTER BUSTER

Talk to your friends

By talking to your friends, you will undoubtedly discover that you're not the only one feeling like this – and seeing your friends talk about their imposter feelings will show you how ridiculous they are. With evidence, make a list of the things you don't feel your doing well enough in. Get three friends to do the same. Then write down what you think each of your friends is doing really well at – this could be a quality ('Your really brave because…') or an achievement ('You wrote a really inspiring blog which made me take action…').

Take it in turns to read out your lists and celebrate each other's accomplishments.

Celebrate your achievements

Write an evidence-based list of your skills and successes. Put a copy of these up somewhere you can see them on a daily basis.

Keep positive feedback

Write down any positive feedback given to you in emails, cards or verbally; particularly feedback that gives evidence to support the praise. On bad days refer back to the list, read through this evidence, and celebrate who you are, what you have already achieved and the positive impact you have had.

PERFECTIONISM

A compulsive drive to be flawless and the setting of unattainably high standards and goals (perfectionism) often goes hand in hand with imposter syndrome. Perfectionism is then combined with harsh self-criticism and disappointment and dissatisfaction when you are unable to reach those impossible ideals.

I class myself as a 'recovering perfectionist'. Some psychologists believe there is a healthy version of this – 'striving for excellence'. This may be so, but in my practice I see numerous clients who are unable to cope with mistakes and failure – anything that they feel makes them 'imperfect'.

So why do some of us feel the need to be perfect? It's a mixture of neuroscience and how we were raised. When we are afraid, part of our brain (the amygdala) triggers the release of chemicals that results in the 'fight-flight-freeze' response. This reaction helps to keep us safe when faced with physical danger, but we experience the same response when we make a mistake – we are afraid how others will react.

In addition to this natural brain response, how we were raised directly influences the *degree* to which we berate ourselves. So the extent to which we were reprimanded or punished for getting something wrong, and how much success we had to achieve to gain praise and love, will determine our levels of self-punishment in adult life.

You can see how all of this might affect you on a practical level: beneath the surface perfectionism also causes anxiety, depression and even eating disorders and body dysmorphia (because of the need to be physically 'perfect' and to be in control at all times). Perfectionism has been linked to OCD, social phobia, workaholism, self-harm and substance abuse, as well as to physical

'Perfection is not a prerequisite for anything but pain.'

DANNA FAULDS

SYMPTOMS OF PERFECTIONISM

These are pretty far-reaching, and there are many I have worked on with my clients to overcome. They include:

- The feeling that you can never reach where you want to be.

- Spending hours and hours trying to get something 'right'.

- Procrastinating or not being able to finish something – both stemming from the fear of not getting it 'perfect'.

- The feeling that you 'fail' at everything you try.

- Not being able to take compliments or acknowledge your own 'successes' because you feel you could have done better.

- Struggling to relax or switch off because you are thinking about what's next or how to do things better.

- Constantly working and achieving, or thinking about work – often at the expense of relationships, your own wellbeing and physical health.

illnesses such as chronic stress and heart disease. Studies have found that perfectionists have a higher than usual mortality rate due to the additional stress and worry caused by the belief that everything should be perfect. The pursuit of perfection will stop you from living a full and happy life. If you want to the break the cycle there are three key steps you can take:

01. Set realistic goals

Perfectionists can find it difficult to distinguish between achievable goals and fantastical ones that only lead to angst when they are not reached. Going for unachievable goals can also lead you to push yourself beyond healthy, sustainable levels. By setting excessive targets, you activate the fight-flight-freeze response. By lowering your goal levels to those that are actually achievable without stress or anxiety, you take yourself out of panic mode and back to a state where the front of your brain – the part that is concerned with strategic thinking and problem-solving – is engaged. You will actually get more done, and do it far more successfully because your brain is functioning at a higher level.

02. Practise and celebrate failing

Failure is an unacceptable word for a perfectionist, but failure is not a measure of your worth, it is actually an essential part of learning, growth and development. One of *the* most effective ways to beat the pressures of perfectionism is to learn a new skill or to do something that takes a lot of patience and trial and error – and yes, to get things wrong along the way.

When we step out of our comfort zones, we make mistakes. Every time you mess up or don't hit the mark – celebrate it – it means you are growing and learning.

03. Accept who you are

Remember that if no one explicitly accepted, acknowledged or celebrated who you are when you were growing up, you may have turned to achievement as the measure of your self-worth. Consequently, the best antidote for perfectionism (and the most challenging) is to be brave enough to just *be* your unpolished imperfect self – with all of your flaws, faults and limitations. By accepting who you really are, with some self-compassion, you can free yourself up to be *your* best version, and to succeed. I only ask that you separate out these old beliefs – your 'successes' are not who you are. 'Achievement' is not a measure of your worth! You are perfectly flawed, and perfectly wonderful all at the same time – as we all are.

PERFECTION DIAL-DOWN

The next time you take on a task or project, choose one of the steps below, and the following time try another one.

Instead of going for a 10/10 in achievement and effort, purposefully go for an 8/10 – whatever that looks like to you. Notice and write down the effects – are they positive or negative? Notice the difference in the amount of time and energy spent on the task.

Make a mistake (yes, I know how difficult this one is).
But do it, and write down the impact and effects.

The next time you make a 'mistake', or you 'fail', shift your mindset from one where you tell yourself, 'I'm an idiot', 'How could I have been so stupid?', 'How could I get that wrong?', to one where you ask, 'What can I learn from this?' Write down a few positive suggestions to help you reframe a new mindset.

When you find yourself slipping into 'perfection anxiety' let go of what *you haven't yet done,* stop worrying about what you still have to do, and come back to 'now' – the present moment. Value the 'now'. Make a list of all the things you've already achieved that day – however small.

SELF-COMPASSION

Instead of being hard on yourself and being critical of your mistakes or failings, learning self-compassion will allow you to be kind, forgiving and sympathetic towards yourself when you *do* fall short.

There is no such thing as 'perfect' (we are all fabulously flawed human beings) and self-compassion is about acknowledging that and allowing ourselves to be what we are – human.

When a friend tells you they've done something wrong or stupid, you don't say, 'You're so stupid!' How could you have done that? What were you thinking?' Instead you feel empathy for them and their suffering (the word compassion literally means 'to suffer together'). Rather than judging or criticizing their actions, you offer kindness and understanding, 'Yes, maybe that wasn't the best thing to do, but next time you'll do it better. You are not the first person to have made a mistake – you're only human!'

Self-compassion involves doing the same for ourselves as we would for others:

noticing that we are suffering; feeling kindness and caring towards *ourselves*; and realizing that *we are* only human too.

When I first introduce this concept to my high-achieving, outwardly successful clients, many are resistant to it – believing it to be self-pitying rubbish that will prevent them from achieving what they want in life. They fully believe that self-criticism is essential to keep them motivated, creating the next big thing and smashing through the next barrier. They are afraid that if they let go of all their self-criticism, they will no longer be motivated to be successful in life.

One client recently said: 'Yes, but if I did that – if I was 'kind' to myself (and they literally said this with a sneer, like it was dirty word) – instead of driving myself harder and harder, I would just stop, give up,

> ### 'We are not the survival of the fittest, we are the survival of the nurtured.'
>
> LOUIS COZOLINO

and end up in a dead-end job. I would give up on everything, I would end up going nowhere!' This isn't being self compassionate, it is being self-pitying and self-sabotaging – the sort of behaviour that makes us feel worse about ourselves rather than better, and less able to move forward and change things. In contrast, being self-compassionate is about doing what's *best* for your health and happiness – not only at this moment, but also in the long run.

In fact, far from being demotivating, self-compassion is *more* motivating than self-criticism. When you show yourself compassion, forgiveness and kindness, you become *more* responsible for your actions, not less. Several studies have shown that the more self-compassionate we are, the more able we are to achieve our goals, the more resilient we are in times of stress, that we are less reactive and angry, and that we enjoy life more as we do achieve. As I say to my clients, self-compassion gives you the ability to *love the life you have, while you create the life of your dreams*. Studies have also shown that practising self-compassion can actually alter our nervous system and body chemistry – from being anxious and hyper-vigilant to danger, to being calmer and more contented. Conversely, they have also shown that the more self-critical we are, the *less* likely we are to achieve our goals.

To sum up, when you are self-compassionate, you become able to make the changes in your life that are the best for you. You start to honour and celebrate who you are as a human being; you are more forgiving of yourself; and more able to pick yourself up, dust yourself off, and carry on regardless – in spite of any mistakes or failures along the way. You will be more able to feel and believe that you *are* 'good enough' and that there is no such thing as 'perfect' – you are just human, and a work-in-progress like the rest of us.

BUILDING SELF-COMPASSION

The problem with being hard on yourself is it becomes ingrained and automatic that most of the time you will barely notice it is happening. So, the first thing you need to do is start catching yourself when you do it. Take some time to think about how you can build self-compassion.

Notice and record

A good place to start is to take an inventory of the most common things you say to yourself. For example, 'You should have worked harder on that', 'Why didn't you know that?' The list is endless but when you start to record these instances, you will notice a theme or a number of regular self-judgements.

What's the kindest thing you can say to yourself?

Start replacing each criticism with a dose of motivating self-compassion –
something you *would* say to a close friend. Phrases such as:
'That was a really tough situation, you did do your best with what you had/knew at the
time.' 'Okay, I may not have done great there, but what's the learning for next time?'
'I love and accept myself exactly as I am.'
'I am just human and a work in progress like everyone else.'
Or my favourite:
'What's the kindest thing I can do for myself/say to myself at this moment?'

Comfort yourself

When we are hard on ourselves we go into a flight-flight-freeze response – we will be
feeling anxious because of the stress hormone cortisol that is pumping through our body.
A great way to come out of that negative, judging place (and into a kinder, more
motivating one) is to physically comfort yourself. I learned this technique from the
queen of self-compassion Kristin Neff, in her book *Self Compassion*. She says that by
doing something she calls a Hugging Practice, we literally self-soothe our way out of the
flight-flight-freeze response, and all of the self-judgement that brings. Hugging releases
oxytocin in the brain, which immediately reduces stress levels and makes us feel calm,
content, trusting and secure.

The next time this happens, give yourself a hug. If there are people around, or you are in
a meeting, you can wrap your arms around one another in a way that is not too obvious,
and give yourself a squeeze. And if even that is not possible, you can imagine hugging
yourself, and this will also give that immediate calming effect.

SELF-ACKNOWLEDGEMENT

What are you celebrating in your life right now? Take a minute to think. Pausing to reflect on and celebrate our achievements before we move onto the next thing is not something we do often, but just for now, have a go.

When we find something to celebrate, 'I did manage to do a good presentation', etc., we commonly focus on external things or our actions, and often we put those down to 'luck': 'Oh I was just lucky, I had a friendly crowd.' It is very rare and actually quite difficult to do a pure self-acknowledgement of who we are as a person and accept that this is what led to the achievement in the first place. Your good presentation was not down to luck – it was down to your courage, tenacity, integrity (or another key quality of yours).

Self-acknowledgement is the act of recognizing and celebrating a positive quality or trait, or a personal value you are honouring and literally naming it (preferably out loud), so that you can celebrate that part of yourself in that moment. It is a great tool to have in your arsenal to counter negative thoughts. Once you start to do this on a daily basis, you will see a difference in how you think and treat yourself.

As I have mentioned before, self-pride can be received negatively and it is often confused with being arrogant. We are taught to be modest and humble, which often leads us not to accept compliments (let alone direct acknowledgements), if we receive them from others.

We find it hard to accept any kind of acknowledgement because we haven't learned how to be truly proud of ourselves

What am I celebrating in my life, right now?

or how to honour and celebrate our strengths and achievements. Because we are so uncomfortable with this ourselves, when anyone else dares to be 'proud' of who they are or what they've achieved, we often tear them down – either consciously or unconsciously.

If you can celebrate your internal strengths and resources, you will be able to step into them. This is why I often begin my coaching sessions by asking, 'What are you celebrating?' Because amongst all our difficulties it is very easy to forget who we are. When you do acknowledge and celebrate yourself, you start to see yourself differently and become much more able to counteract your negative thoughts and the effects those have on your life. The more you say, 'I am intelligent' the more you will

be able to recognize and live up to that statement. Once you can do this, you will be more able to stay focused and motivated, be better at resolving problems or overcoming obstacles, and be able to achieve what you want in life and enjoy the ride.

Acknowledging your qualities and the personal values you are honouring will also enable you to view events from a more considered and rational viewpoint, because you will have a stronger sense of who you are. Self-acknowledgement can even help you to be less fearful when faced with negative information and events (such as bad news about your physical or mental health) or if you are on the receiving end of prejudice or discrimination, or in any kind of social conflict.

CELEBRATE YOURSELF

Having a vocabulary of words on hand to celebrate yourself and your achievements is a great way to counteract negative thoughts and create a mindset where you can achieve the life you want.

Take a look at the list of words opposite. Every morning ask yourself the question, 'What am I celebrating?' Choose three self-acknowledgements that are true for you (don't worry if you feel embarrassed or don't fully believe them for now. Write them down or circle them. Say your self-acknowledgement words to yourself in a mirror, e.g. 'I am brave'.

At the end of each day think about one thing that has happened, be it good or challenging. Ask yourself, 'Who was I being in that situation?', 'What quality within me enabled that to happen?' Take one quality from the list , or come up with one yourself and write down or repeat the phrase,
'In doing that, I was being [your chosen word], therefore I am [your chosen word].

- → Levelheaded
- → Dependable
- → Grounded
- → Approachable
- → Powerful
- → Active
- → Ambitious
- → Well-meaning
- → Determined
- → Able
- → Tender
- → Articulate
- → Careful
- → Helpful
- → Accessible
- → Spontaneous
- → Authentic
- → Beautiful
- → Discerning
- → Brave
- → Unpretentious
- → Bold
- → Resilient
- → Believable
- → Spiritual
- → Innocent
- → Brilliant
- → Charming
- → Tenacious
- → Clever
- → Mindful
- → Open
- → Confident
- → Sincere
- → Creative

- → Committed
- → Peaceful
- → Intelligent
- → Compassionate
- → Outgoing
- → Caring
- → Outspoken
- → Kind
- → Credible
- → Steady
- → Clear
- → Noble
- → Methodical
- → Outgoing
- → Certain
- → Lovable
- → Capable
- → Shy
- → Courageous
- → Daring
- → Reliable
- → Lucid
- → Distinctive
- → Humble
- → Young at heart
- → Dynamic
- → Wise
- → Diligent
- → Humorous
- → Magnanimous
- → Practical
- → Sound
- → Decisive
- → Quick-witted
- → Vibrant

- → Outrageous
- → Welcoming
- → Detailed
- → Trustworthy
- → Dedicated
- → Likeable
- → Joyous
- → Energetic
- → Strategic
- → Engaging
- → Quirky
- → Grateful
- → Vigilant
- → Fun
- → Serious
- → Fast
- → Frank
- → Flexible
- → Natural
- → Fierce
- → Respectful
- → Strong
- → Polite
- → Gregarious
- → Generous
- → Trusting
- → Laid back
- → Happy
- → Honest
- → Private
- → Visionary
- → Witty
- → Inspiring
- → Qualified
- → Insightful

- → Jovial
- → Keen
- → Unaffected
- → Victorious
- → Learned
- → Thoughtful
- → Original
- → Optimistic
- → Thankful
- → Playful
- → Poised
- → Individual
- → Present
- → Harmonious
- → Exciting
- → Independent
- → Whimsical
- → Responsible
- → Intuitive
- → Soulful
- → Friendly
- → Truthful
- → Mischievous
- → Unique
- → Virtuous
- → Lively
- → Graceful
- → Warm
- → Wry
- → Motivated
- → Youthful
- → Knowing
- → Zesty
- → Patient
- → Joyful

05

COMMIT

From Latin *committere* meaning 'to join' or 'to entrust'; to be dedicated to, pledge or bind to a course of action.

Do you want to make real changes in your life, but wonder where you are going to find the time and energy to do so? Do you feel that taking time for yourself is selfish? Do you find it difficult to say 'no'?

This chapter is designed to help you realize that in order to make any of the changes you want to make in your life, you must make a commitment to your mental and physical health and your general wellbeing. You will learn how to create the time and space to take care of yourself –

challenging and changing the idea that this is a self-indulgent luxury, and instead understanding that this is an essential precursor for any change. You will discover the basic brain science behind and necessity of self-care, as well as the mental and physical costs of not doing so. You will find out why you find it hard to say 'no' and how to start creating healthier boundaries around your time and energy.

BACK TO BASICS

Stress, tiredness, burnout and anxiety are all issues I see a lot. The number-one reason is that people don't take good care of themselves. If this is something you struggle with, you need to focus on self-care before you can even start to think about making any significant changes in your life. You also need to keep a handle on this moving forwards; without addressing the basics – by this I mean exercise, sleep and nutrition – you may as well put this book down right now.

Remember, this is not self-indulgence. When you are running on empty, no one is getting the best of you and there will be physical, mental, emotional and spiritual consequences. Conversely, when we take care of ourselves, we are able to give more to everyone else.

The importance of sleep

A full night's sleep is absolutely vital if you want to stay motivated and make changes in your life. One of the first things I do with my clients is ask how tired they are feeling and how much sleep they are getting.

Nearly all of them *know* they're not getting enough and, because they don't realize the impact of this, they don't prioritize it. In the best-selling book *Why We Sleep*, scientist Matthew Walker highlights just how detrimental sleep deprivation can be, but also how getting *more* sleep can have an immediate, positive effect.

It may be obvious to state that a lack of sleep makes you tired, but crucially, when you are tired you are less motivated. When you experience fatigue you are likely to find yourself doing the bare minimum – anything bigger or more challenging is shunted to the sidelines for another day (if that day ever comes).

A clear head: Sleep deprivation negatively affects the part of your brain responsible for memory, learning and decision-making (the prefrontal cortex or PFC). When we are tired ,the PFC becomes 'foggy', and we find it much harder to learn and retain new information, and to make the best decisions moving forward – all of which are essential elements for effecting change and reaching goals. For that we need a clear head.

Motivation: When we are not getting enough sleep we often become stressed, which can cause our motivation levels and general mood to drop. This negativity can also affect those around us – the people who are often essential to helping or supporting us achieve our work or life goals.

The importance of nutrition

What you eat has a significant impact on your motivation and ability to make changes in your life. According to the World Health Organization, you can actually boost your motivation and overall brain productivity by up to 20 per cent just by eating the right foods. Omega-3 fatty acids play a vital role. They are a key component of the myelin sheath – the protective layer that forms around any new neural pathway developed within the brain. So when you are forming any new behaviour or mindset Omega-3 will help to strengthen the corresponding neural pathway.

Refined carbs and sugar have a negative effect on focus, attention and memory, and have even been linked to depression. Keep these foods to a minimum where possible.

The importance of exercise

When you take regular exercise, (either weights or cardio), three key neurotransmitters are released into your brain. These have a positive effect on your brain and body, as well as on your ability to stay positive and keep motivated.

GABA: The first of these is gamma-aminobutyric acid (GABA). This is a natural tranquillizer and has a calming effect. It can be particularly beneficial if you suffer from stress, or if you're going through a particularly stressful period in your life.

Serotonin: This is the key ingredient of many anti-depressants. Exercise releases serotonin in the brain and will stop you feeling low.

Dopamine: This is the real feel-good hormone that we're often seeking when we eat chocolate, sugar or carbs.

So how do these neurotransmitters help you when changing aspects of your life? The action of these three key brain chemicals, as well as the physical effects of sleep, good food and exercise on your body, will actually make you *feel* differently about yourself and what you can achieve, and you will therefore think differently about what is possible. Your self-esteem will improve, your stress and anxiety levels will fall, and you will feel calmer and more confident. As a consequence, you will be much better able to set targets, keep to them, and achieve your goals.

HERE ARE MY TOP FIVE BOOSTER FOODS

- **Salmon:** High in omega-3 fatty acids (great for improving memory, overall brain performance and relieving depression).

- **Nuts:** High protein, high natural fat content (also good for myelin sheath formation) + amino acids (great for memory and brain function).

- **Berries:** High in antioxidants (good for memory and the prevention of Alzheimer's and Parkinson's disease).

- **Dark chocolate:** High in magnesium (great for lowering stress) + caffeine (helps to focus the mind).

- **Avocados:** Great source of natural fat (good for the brain) + increases blood flow (assists brain function).

And water! We all know our bodies are made up of more than 70 per cent water, and every function in the body and brain depends on water to work effectively. If you want to stay focused, motivated and keep making positive changes in your life, stay hydrated.

THE POWER OF THREE

Sleep

Your sleep schedule can be really difficult to change but this is just because your body is used to the time you currently go to bed; it will adjust to a new, earlier one – it may just take a little while. Try and do the following things:

For the next three weeks create a new sleep schedule and go to bed earlier than you have been (make sure it is the same time every night). Set your alarm for the same time every morning (it helps to do the same at weekends, but do let yourself have a lie-in if you need to).

Nutrition

Cut down on refined carbs and sugars.
Start enjoying my top five booster foods.
Take an omega-3 supplement.

Exercise

Start small. Don't go out and expect to do 30 minutes or an hour straight away.
Build up gradually and that way you will sustain the habit.
Mix it up. If you get bored easily vary what you do.
Find an exercise buddy if being accountable to someone else helps you.
Find a particular class you like, or do your exercise at the same time every day, if you respond well to routine.

Whatever you do, by building up to just 30 minutes of cardio every other day, you are consciously and actively taking a step to change your life, and it will have other positive effects.

MINDFULNESS

Another key ingredient for improving concentration, combatting stress and burnout, and making meaningful and consistent life changes, is mindfulness.

I am not talking about trying to achieve a completely blank or serene mind, or sitting cross-legged like a Buddhist monk, or spending thousands of pounds learning how to 'do it' on a silent retreat. I am talking about practical meditations and exercises that you can use every day – in your home, at work, or even on the bus (and no, you do not have to sit cross-legged to do them).

Why mindfulness?

For me, it means slowing down, taking some long and slow deep breaths and connecting more fully with my body and surroundings. I first started practising mindfulness and then incorporating it in my coaching about four years ago and now it is an integral part of my work.

Over the past sixty years, extensive scientific research and numerous studies have shown that mindfulness can play an important role in improving mental performance, regulating emotions, and reducing stress levels. It boosts mental performance by increasing the grey matter in the brain – the most notable area involved in learning and memory. It also creates changes in the white matter, which regulates how you behave and act on emotions and impulses. It has been shown to reduce the levels of the stress hormones cortisol and adrenaline in the body, thereby reducing overall anxiety levels.

The benefits of practising mindfulness include reducing the symptoms of depression, increasing performance and improving self-esteem. In the workplace, particularly in challenging work environments, it has also been found to reduce stress levels and cases of burnout,

> '**Mindfulness means paying attention in a particular way: on purpose, in the present moment, and non-judgementally.**'
>
> JON KABAT-ZINN

leading to reduced staff turnover levels. In children, it's been shown to increase resilience and even to help them deal with bullies. Mindfulness has been shown to be particularly helpful if you:

- have anxiety and worries
- have low energy levels
- have poor concentration levels
- feel irritable
- are easily annoyed and argumentative
- feel joyless and unmotivated.

Practising mindfulness on a regular basis has been shown to:

- improve concentration and memory
- control anger and negative emotions
- lower blood pressure and heart rate
- improve immune function
- increase self-awareness
- provide clarity of thought and perspective
- provide a sense of calm and connectedness

There are two ways you can practise mindfulness in everyday life:

Mindful meditation is an inward-looking practice that usually has a particular focus. For this I typically recommend starting with an app, and there are plenty on the market for beginners. Find one that has short meditations of ten minutes to make it easy for you to include it in your daily life.

Mindful living is an outward practice and often an easier one to start with. It's a way of including mindfulness in everyday actions. It means slowing down and paying full attention, being in the moment and focusing on the action itself, your body movements and emotions, as well as the sights, sounds, sensations, smells and even tastes involved.

You will reap the benefits of mindfulness if you practise it regularly for about eight weeks or more. Studies have shown that just ten minutes of mindfulness daily can lead to better self-regulation and better brain function – especially in the areas of attention and memory. To include mindfulness in your daily routine, I recommend considering the following:

01. Routine
I highly recommend meditating as a daily practice (preferably incorporated into a morning routine as detailed in the next section). Do it in the same place at the same time, and follow a set routine of preparation – this will make it easier to stick to.

02. Location
The place and environment in which you meditate is hugely important. Wherever you choose, make sure you won't be interrupted and make sure it is clear of clutter, has minimal noise and is comfortable. I started off sitting on my bed but have since moved outside into my garden (even during the winter), where I meditate under a blanket and with the light of a rechargeable camping light for those dark mornings.

03. Posture
Make sure your back is upright with your chin slightly lowered. Relax your shoulders, open your chest, but don't slouch or curve your spine. This is important to allow energy to flow up and down your body.

Ideally, you should sit without back support and cross-legged, but if you have lower back problems, use support and sit with your legs stretched out in front of you.

Mindful living exercises
You can increase your daily mindfulness whatever your schedule by simply doing what you were already doing, but in a mindful way. The ways in which you can incorporate mindfulness into your daily life are pretty endless. I suggest you start small, by trying one regular activity per day, and seeing which one works best for you. Here are a few examples to get you going:

- Brushing your teeth
- Showering or washing your hair
- Making a cup of tea or coffee
- Eating
- Walking to work
- Noticing your body posture
- Driving
- Gardening
- Working out
- Drawing or any creative activity
- Having a conversation
- Washing up
- Preparing for sleep

MINI MINDFULNESS

Close your eyes and take some long, slow, deep breaths, breathing in through your nose, holding it, then breathing out through your mouth. Inhale the breath right down into your stomach. You may notice your mind wandering off. If you do, gently, without judgement, bring your attention back to your breath.

Take this time to fully focus on your body. Notice if there's one place in your body that is calling for your attention. Go there and really get curious. Take a couple of long, slow breaths right down into this place. Notice if anything happens to it as you do. No judgement, just noticing. Now take a couple more deep breaths and shift your attention, seeking out a place in your body that's 'silent' right now – a place you really have to go looking for. Again, when you find it, go there and get curious. Breathe right down into it, filling it up with new fresh air. Notice what happens to it as you do so.

Taking your attention back out to your whole body, notice the overriding emotion. Take a moment to stretch your boday. Bring your focus behind your eyelids and pause for a moment. Open your eyes and adjust to the light when you are ready.

What did you notice?

02

What was the overriding emotion in your body?

MORNING ROUTINES

The most effective way to change your life on a daily basis is to start an early morning routine. This will provide immediate momentum and motivation to conquer the rest of the day.

Every morning you will have time to think about and focus on your goals and the kind of life you want. Before most people have woken up, you will be giving yourself small victories and this will affect the rest of your day; you will be proactive instead of reactive.

A morning routine will give you up to two, possibly even three, hours a day to focus completely on yourself. Once you take the leap and start to get up earlier, you will see results; you may even decide to push the time back even further to give yourself more uninterrupted space to work and focus on the things you *really* want to be doing. This investment will also pay off during the rest of the day – when you have already made a head start with your goals, you will feel much more positive and motivated for the entire day.

It is well known that some of the most successful and wealthiest people in the world do or have done this. They all attribute much of their success and focus to their morning routine – Barack Obama, Anna Wintour and Steve Jobs, to name a few. You probably don't have staff, or full-time childcare, so how on earth can you do this on top of everything else?

Studies show that morning people are likely to be much more driven and productive. Research also shows that stress will dramatically affect your productivity throughout the day, as well as your overall wellbeing. Starting your day with a structured morning routine of exercise, meditation and reflection will seriously reduce your stress levels all round, so as well as getting stuff done, you will also

be positively affecting your overall mood and wellbeing for the rest of the entire day.

After reading Hal Elrod's book *The Miracle Morning*, I have had my own morning routine for three years now. I started out just getting up at 6.30am instead of 7am, but I enjoyed it so much that my wake-up time is now 5.30am – trust me, I never thought I'd ever be getting up at this time voluntarily!

Three years later, I absolutely attribute what I'm doing now to those extra hours I gained each morning. Since starting my morning routine, I have read a stack of books I never would have had time to get through – books that support my learning and growth as a coach and as a business woman. I have been able to launch my blog and YouTube channel. I have also conquered my stop-start habit of exercising, and generally I just feel better, both physically and emotionally, because I am focusing on me and my life, every single day. On the following page is my morning routine – I do it every day but relax the times a bit at weekends.

MY MORNING ROUTINE

→ **5.30am**
Alarm. Glass of water, open curtains and window.
Brush teeth, splash face with cold water.
Make pot of coffee.

→ **5.40am**
Meditate.

→ **6am**
Journal (gratitudes, acknowledgements, three things I want to achieve/experience that day), speak to partner.

→ **6.15am**
Read (self-help book or specialist subject book)/write.

→ **6.45am**
Daughter wakes up, I make her breakfast and hang out.

→ **7.15am**
Go running / do a HIIT session / get ready.

→ **8am**
Leave house.

Creating a morning routine

The whole function of a morning routine is to set your own focus for the day – rather than allowing that focus to be set for you by all of those outside responsibilities and pressures. The idea is to create a set of habits that will transform your life on a daily basis.

Habit 1: get up!
The first habit to establish is that you actually get up when your alarm goes off – this was the hardest one for me. What really helps here is a big glass of water (dehydration makes you feel sleepy) and opening the curtains. So that is the first step – no snooze button!

Habit 2: meditate
I've used a variety of meditation apps to help myself get going. Do shop around and try out different ones before settling on what works for you. Scientists have shown that meditation really does have a positive impact on the brain. It will give you the clarity, focus and motivation you'll need to make changes, as well as help to reduce stress and anxiety.

Habit 3: journal
This is extremely good for reflecting on and thinking about what is important

> 'Focused, productive, successful mornings generate focused, productive, successful days – which inevitably create a successful life – in the same way that unfocused, unproductive, and mediocre mornings generate unfocused, unproductive, and mediocre days, and ultimately a mediocre quality of life. By simply changing the way you wake up in the morning, you can transform any area of your life, faster than you ever thought possible.'
>
> HAL ELROD

to you on a daily basis. It also helps you keep track of what you're doing and your achievements along the way. My journal practise comprises three gratitudes, three self-acknowledgments and three things I want for the day.

Habit 4: read
I have found this has made a huge difference; if you read for 30 minutes every day, think how quickly that adds up.

Habit 5: exercise
I found this tough, especially in the cold. As I've said, it immediately makes you feel more focused and motivated, and is great for combatting stress and anxiety.

Habit 6: practise visualization
The other great step that will help you stay on track is visualization. Set a timer on your phone (ten minutes is ideal, five minutes is enough to start with), and just sit there with your eyes closed and imagine your goal and the kind of life you want to be creating.

SAYING 'NO'

This is an issue I see again and again with my clients. If, like my clients, you struggle with the idea of prioritizing your self-care over everyone else's needs, then read on.

Saying 'no' is about creating healthy boundaries around your time and energy; it is not about being *mean* or *selfish* or disregarding the wants or needs of others. However, it can be extremely difficult, because we have a very deep fear of rejection. If early humans were cast out by their tribe, they wouldn't survive; today even though our lives are not actually at stake, we worry that if we say 'no' people will be disappointed in us, angry with us, or that we will have hurt their feelings. Moreover (and this is more common for women), many of us were raised to be 'nice' or 'kind', and to put the needs of others before ourselves, and these beliefs remain with us into adulthood. A fear of rejection combined with a tendency to put others

first leads to a high likelihood of our saying 'yes' to everything. So let's start looking at how you can begin saying 'no' well, and not feeling 'bad' or 'wrong' in the process.

Prioritize and schedule

We all only have so many hours in the day and so much that needs to get done during that time. In addition, we often have long-term dreams and goals we want to fulfill. If we want to sustain all of this *and* live a happy, balanced life, we must take time out to take care of ourselves and enjoy it all (otherwise what's the point?).

Sit down and prioritize – schedule into your calendar or diary, whatever you use – everything that *you* need and want to be doing. For example, if a nice long dog walk first thing in the morning sets you up for the day, schedule that in. If going out with your friends once a week makes you happy, schedule it in. If you want Saturdays to be a day set aside completely for you and your loved one or family, yes, schedule it in.

Then, if someone asks you to do something during that time, you have a valid reason to say no – it's in your calendar. Doing this really helps with any doubts and decision-making, and with any potential guilt. You and your life are important.

Rehearse

The way you deliver your 'no' is important. Research shows that when we make a specific plan before we do something, we are far more likely to do it – in the way we intended. So rehearse! There will be certain people in your life who constantly ask for help or to whom you find it difficult to say 'no'. Start with them and rehearse a simple, direct, but polite response. For example:

'I really appreciate you asking, but my week is completely full and I can't take on anything else at the moment.'

Because this is true – your calendar is full. You can offer a compromise – but only if you really want to – such as:

'I'm sorry I can't spend time helping you to write that article – but here's a blog I wrote on how to get started.'

Focus on the positives

Once you've done that, rather than feeling that you are a 'bad' person, be aware that there is nothing 'good' about doing something with resentment or anger. People will feel more comfortable around you knowing that your 'no' means no, and that when you do say 'yes' you really mean it and want to help them – this all creates trust.

You have also made a conscious decision and taken action to create a better life for yourself – and your loved ones. Be sure to celebrate who you are in saying 'no'. Doing that and reclaiming your time is hard work and really brave. Acknowledge what you have given yourself – time, energy, space – to do the things that are really important.

CREATING NEW MINDSETS

If you really want to make a change in your life or break any old habits or behaviours that may be holding you back, then you need to understand what is happening in your brain when you try (and often fail) to make those changes.

When you are trying to break an old pattern of thinking, feeling or behaving, you are creating a new neural pathway in your brain. I see it like a woodland pathway – in order for that pathway to become a well-trodden route, you need to walk down it again and again. When you are creating any new habit (for example, getting up early to run in the morning), you are not only creating a brand new pathway, but you are *also* having to resist the urge to go down an already well-trodden, easier pathway (staying in your nice warm bed). This all takes a lot of brain energy and effort.

These patterns are laid down in the prefrontal cortex or PFC; this is the part of the brain that is concerned with conscious thought, strategizing, goal-setting and motivation. It only has a certain amount of energy available at the beginning of each day, so when you are tired or stressed, or just have too much on, there is not enough energy left to create new habits. This is when your brain reverts to the limbic system, which controls our instinct for survival. It is automatic and uses much less energy but in this state there is little chance of making the best decisions or creating any new habits. Change requires a *lot* of energy, attention and consistency, so when you don't allow for that, you will not succeed. On the following pages are some suggestions of how to create new and lasting habits.

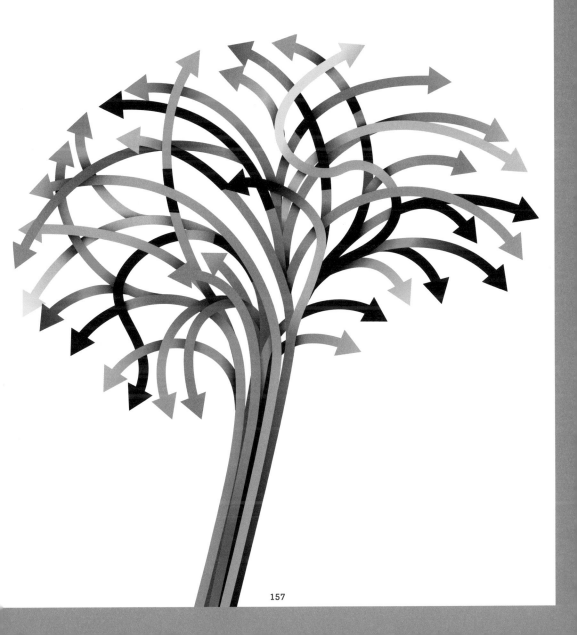

> '**Commitment is the little choices every day that lead to the final results we're striving for.**'
>
> ANON

01. Create space and reduce stress

Clear the decks and let go of something – whatever is using up your brain energy. Remember, your brain only has so much capacity each day and there are only a certain number of hours. For every new thing you take on, get into the habit of asking yourself what you can let go of. Aim to perform any new actions in the morning or after a break to minimize the amount of 'mental load' on the brain. In addition, take care of the basics – sleep, exercise and nutrition – in order to reduce stress.

02. Focus on the benefits

Being human, you will naturally avoid situations that cause pain or discomfort and seek out the ones that give you pleasure. This is another ancient survival mechanism, which at its most basic level, is designed to keep you safe. It does not care whether you live a happy and fulfilled life – just that you are physically alive.

If you really want your brain to make the extra effort to create a new neural pathway, you need to focus on the benefits and the pleasures it will bring you. Using that early morning run as an example, focus your mind on the high it will give you, how good you will feel about having done it, and how much better you'll look (if that's your goal). You will also need to stop focusing on the bad – the aches and pains, the cold mornings, the perceived monotony – this all takes practise!

List the benefits, gains and pleasures of creating a new habit and put them up somewhere you will see them every day. Create a vision board of what your life will look like as a result of this new habit. Regularly reward yourself for performing your new behaviour – psychologists call this *positive reinforcement*. If the habit itself doesn't bring natural rewards, add in an extra feel-good factor – such as putting your feet up and reading your favourite magazine afterwards. Also, be clear on the drawbacks of *not* making or creating this change – what it will cost you. For example, if you don't stop smoking, you may not be around to see your kids grow up. When I was in my twenties, a doctor did this very effectively. He told me that if I didn't quit smoking, as an asthmatic, I would be living in hospital in an oxygen tent by the time I was 40. It worked!

03. Keep in familiar

When they are ready to commit to their new behaviour, most of my clients want to go all-out: 'I will go to the gym five days a week for an hour – at 6am every morning.' Every time I hear this, I have to stop them in their tracks and reel them back in so that they start with something smaller and more manageable. This is because doing anything *too* new or *too* scary activates the amygdala (commonly known as an amygdala hijack), which pushes us back to our old, 'safe', known ways of operating – or 'homeostasis' as it is called by neuroscientists. When this happens, we are unable to evaluate the situation rationally, or make the best life decisions.

It is helpful for your brain in that moment not to have to make any difficult decisions or think too much about any new behaviour. This is why doing something every day is much better than having to ask yourself, 'Is this a day on or a day off from my new habit?' Doing something at the same time in the same place is also extremely helpful as it makes your brain feel 'safe'.

04. Make changes gradually

To avoid activating the amygdala, we therefore need to implement any change or new habit in small and regular steps, and stick to a familiar routine. For example, when starting a new exercise routine, it is much better to start with 15 minutes of running every day instead of aiming for much longer runs. It is also best to keep the situation or location as similar as possible, to give your brain the feeling of familiarity and safety that it needs.

05. Allow plenty of time

Depending on what else your brain is dealing with, and the difficulty or complexity of your new habit, you will need to allow plenty of time for it to become your 'new normal'. There are a number of theories about how much time this takes but my very rough estimate is to allow at least three months of *consistent* effort (again – a small, daily action is preferable to sporadic large acts) for any new behaviour. Remember, during that time you will need keep your stress levels down, stay focused on the benefits, and make the action as easy and familiar as possible.

> '**Commitment leads to action.**
> **Action brings your dream closer.**'
>
> MARICA WIEDER

You may be replacing a very well-trodden old behaviour of 30–40 years, so this will take time. Allow for this, be patient, and give yourself all the help you can. Create a system where this change is being supported and rewarded for at least the three months I've suggested. Schedule and monitor your new behaviour or habit – the same time every day is best. Smartwatches, activity trackers and apps with rewards along the way are all great for keeping you motivated. Be accountable – publicly via social media, or on a smaller scale within a group if that works for you. Alternatively, buddy up with a friend or someone else wanting to achieve the same thing as you. If you do all of this and the change is really important to you but you still feel blocked by something you just can't identify, then seek some personal support through coaching, therapy or group therapy – whatever it is you need to make this permanent change in your life.

Staying motivated

If motivation is a problem for you, then you need to acquaint yourself with the Kim Kardashian of neurotransmitters – dopamine. It is dubbed as such because it's the sexy hormone – the one we're all chasing through addictions such as caffeine, alcohol, sugar, shopping, sex and gambling – things that give us a high.

It is also known as the 'motivation molecule' because it boosts levels of drive, focus and attention. With low levels of dopamine you will feel a lack of joy and zest for life; you won't feel motivated to do or achieve much at all, and you will be prone to procrastination and apathy.

Many of us have low levels of dopamine due to poor diet and nutrition. It's made from the amino acid L-tyrosine which is commonly found in protein-rich foods, such as almonds, avocados, bananas, eggs, beef and chicken, as well as in dark chocolate, coffee and green tea. Alongside what we eat, what we do can also have a huge effect on our dopamine levels. Top dopamine-boosting activities include exercise; sex and physical contact; meditation; listening to music (dancing to music will give you a double boost); and creative hobbies, such as crafting and knitting.

Focusing on the benefits

As I have said before, as humans we are hard-wired for pleasure – it's our brain's way of getting us to do things to survive. That is why eating, sex and making money all trigger dopamine, which controls our brain's pleasure/reward centre. What will motivate us and keep us motivated, is focusing on the benefits of what we want to achieve, the good stuff we will get as a result of all of this effort and energy (dopamine is also released after any effort we put in).

For example, in one of my early *Change Your Life in 5* videos you can see me put all of this to the test by attempting to get into the North Sea for the first time in winter. For this task I focused on how I would feel if I completed the challenge. I did my research and knew that I'd gain the added benefit of a natural high via a shot of endorphins, serotonin and dopamine. I also knew it was thought to be good for my immune system, great for skin and cellulite, and was said to improve your sex life by releasing an extra

dose of oestrogen. All of this helped me in the moment when my skin came into contact with that very cold North Sea water!

If what you are wanting to achieve isn't that rewarding in itself (but just has to be done), then add on something that is – and that will give you that helpful boost.

Making it easy

Your brain constantly evaluates how rewarding and how difficult *something is* – so to effectively control your brain you need to make whatever you're doing feel as easy as possible.

As part of my preparation for going into the North Sea, I bought myself some neoprene gloves and booties to keep my hands and feet from freezing, and on the day my partner made a fire on the beach to sit in front of as soon as we got out.

This is why people talk about breaking things down into small, manageable chunks and just taking one small step at a time – if you make something easier you will actually do it.

DESIGN YOUR LIFE – THE MASTER PLAN

Now you are equipped with the five core principles of *how* to make permanent, meaningful changes in your life, it's time for the *doing* bit. Having read and worked through the exercises in this book, it is always helpful to have a master plan, together with the support you need, to help you make it all happen.

Create a clear vision

It is important to have a clear, compelling vision to keep returning to – both for when times get hard or challenging and to simply remind you of where you're headed. So, once you have clarified your ideal life (see the exercise on pages 34–37) it's useful to put into the context of a longer-term plan, with goals and targets to hit along the way. When I do this with clients, we typically plan for two years ahead. I find this far enough in the future to stop you being overwhelmed, but close enough to create reachable goals you can aim for consistently. Even once you have made a

plan, you can still be open and flexible to whatever comes up along the way. Having a clear, compelling vision acts as a great compass – if you don't have one it is all too easy to lose focus and motivation, and to give up because change starts to feel too hard. However, if you break actions down into smaller, achievable targets and goals, you are much more likely to stay on track, and keep going when things get tough (which they invariably will).

Either keep the vision of your long-term goal in written form or, as I do and many of my clients prefer, create a vision board – on or offline. A vision board is simply a

> '**If you are working on something exciting that you really care about, you don't have to be pushed. The vision pulls you.**'
>
> STEVE JOBS

visual representation of the end goal, and includes images and words that represent the various elements and values you will be honouring.

I created a vision board to keep me focused on my big goal during a very challenging time. My daughter and I had been forced to leave our lovely rental house after three years. It was particularly heartbreaking because it had been our first home for just the two of us following my split from her father. We'd really made it our own and we loved living there. It was just round the corner from her school and very close to all our friends. Due to a rise in rental prices, we had to move further out and to a much smaller flat – all for more money. It was at this point, reeling from the shock (and lack of choice), that I decided I wanted to create a more permanent, stable home for us both, but I realized I needed to save up a considerable amount of money for a mortgage deposit to do so. Weighing up all our options, I decided to bite the bullet, and we both moved into a close friend's spare room, from where I also ran my business. This lasted for just under a year. During this difficult time, I found creating and referring to my vision board extremely helpful. It is such a reminder of what I can

'I love the life I have while I create the life of my dreams.'

HAL ELROD

cope with and achieve that I had it framed and it now hangs in my office.

Targets and goals

Setting incremental goals and targets on the way to your end vision is essential. Smaller more manageable goals will help you stay on track.

First, imagine yourself in two years' time, living your vision – make it as detailed as possible. Then create an imaginary timeline: count down and detail the targets you need to hit along the way. Ask yourself more and more questions and go into as much detail as you can. As you progress, this will enable you to look back and see what is possible.

Block off time in your calendar

If it's not scheduled, it's just not going to happen. This is an issue for us all – it's just how our brains are wired. If we don't schedule in our exercise, if we don't set an alarm to go to bed early (and get up the next morning for a run), if we don't set aside time to buy in the right foods, our good intentions get sidelined by the day-to-day tasks in hand. Scientists call it 'Present Bias'. It means we are hard-wired for immediate, quick wins, and will naturally avoid the harder, longer-term effort that bigger changes often require. Make what you need or want to change a priority. Once you've decided what you need to take care of – whether it's researching your next steps, speaking to people to get more information, or getting more sleep to help you do it all – schedule in the time to do it. Make these time slots non-negotiable.

Or, as I say to many of my clients 'Make yourself your number-one client', protecting these time slots and not giving them up whatever happens. Guard them with your life, because actually, your life does depend upon it. During these blocks of time, if you have the three basics handled – sleep, exercise and nutrition – you can start adding in time for any other kind of rejuvenating activity (such as sitting quietly for ten minutes, listening to music, reading an inspiring book or enjoying a funny TV show) whatever gives you rest and reward, and keeps you motivated.

Seek support

You don't have to do this alone. Change is hard, and it can often be harder when you're struggling by yourself. Depending on your personality, you may thrive more in a group, or in a one-on-one setting (I'm a one-on-one girl). Be aware of what has worked for you in the past, and make sure you get the right support. You may also want help from an expert – someone who can help you dig deeper, hold you accountable, and help you overcome any fears doubts or insecurities that may be holding you back. To this day, I have a coach and mentor who supports me in fulfilling my dreams and goals, who is there to call me out when I am holding myself back, and who stops me being small in life.

YOUR VISION BOARD

Create your clear, compelling vision using a big piece of card, scissors, glue and images. Date your vision, plus your targets and goals along the way. You can do this by recording the details on your phone, making notes as you go, or you can use the template below.

(01)

Vision and date

(typically 2 years from now)

Vision board – written details

1 year targets and date:

6 months targets and date:

4 months targets and date:

2 months targets and date:

1 month targets and date:

2 weeks targets and date:

NEXT STEPS

Congratulations on reading this book, taking the steps towards achieving a rich, fulfilling life, and starting to make conscious choices about how you live it. Please do take a moment to acknowledge the qualities within you that have got you to this point.

There are several resources that can support you if you get stuck. They will allow you to get back on track and make meaningful changes in your life:

Online

At the time of writing, I am creating an online portal for readers of this book. It will contain downloadable versions of all of the exercises, audio versions of the visualizations, and you will also be able to connect with others who are on a similar journey.

I will also be launching a monthly membership for additional tools and content, live private webinars with me, and e-learning modules – all to further support you on your journey. Please do sign up for the waitlist and be first to know when I open the doors: www.suebelton.com/bookresources

Coaching programmes

I have two signature coaching programmes – *Back on Track* for privately funded individuals and *The Conscious Leader*, an organization-sponsored coaching programme. Both are six-month programmes designed to help professionals, leaders and founders implement best-life and leadership practices.

They are designed to help you practise and apply the five key steps in this book in a way that's completely personalized to you, your life, and any challenges you might face. You will get goal-focused accountability, and one-to-one, 24-hour support from me every single step of the way.

Since 2008, hundreds of people have worked with me through these programmes to dramatically challenge and shift old ways of thinking and behaving, to take back control of their lives and careers, and to start living rich, fulfilling lives.

Back on Track and *The Conscious Leader* provide personalized tools and techniques to deepen and speed up your progress. I have discovered that personalized strategies offer faster results with greater impact.

The programmes run globally via zoom, and face-to-face at my coaching rooms in Wimpole Street and St Paul's, London. The process requires time and commitment because of the learning and implementation required. My clients consistently tell me that the programme, and working with me in this way, has helped them make dramatic improvements and changes in their life – far beyond what they ever dreamed was possible.

For more information on the *Back on Track and The Conscious Leader* visit: www.suebelton.com

To download a *Back on Track* brochure go to: https://suebelton.com/Back-On-Track-Brochure.pdf

Connect

At the beginning of the book you will have read how my life's purpose is to help others see that they always have a choice and can always make changes in their lives – even when they don't feel they can. I would love to hear your experiences of this. How you are implementing what you've taken from this book and any changes you make. I would especially love to hear your celebrations – of who you are, as well as your achievements.

You can connect with me on:

Facebook: Change Your Life in 5
Instagram: @changeyourlifein5
LinkedIn: Sue Belton

INDEX

REFERENCES

CHAPTER 1: CLARIFY
Pages 22-25: Maslow, Abraham. 'A Theory of Human Motivation', *Psychological Review* 50, no. 4 (1943): 370-396.

Page 53: CTI (Co-Active Training Institute). 'Life Purpose Vizualization'. Published here by permission. No reproduction, in any form, printed or electronic, is permitted without prior permission from CTI.

CHAPTER 2: CONQUER
Page 72: Kajitani, Shinya, *et al. 'Use It Too Much and Lose It*? The Effect of Working Hours on Cognitive Ability'. Melbourne Institute Working Paper No. 7/16 (February, 2016). ISSN 1328-4991 (Print); ISSN 1447-5863 (Online); ISBN 978-0-7340-4405-1.

Page 76: CTI (Co-Active Training Institute). 'Future Self exercise'. Published here by permission. No reproduction, in any form, printed or electronic, is permitted without prior permission from CTI.

CHAPTER 3: CHOOSE
Pages 97-101: CTI (Co-Active Training Institute). 'Balance Formula'.

Whitworth, Laura, *et al. Co-Active Coaching: Changing Business Transforming Lives* (Nicholas Brealey Publishing, 2011).

Cuddy, Amy. 'Your Body Language Shapes Who You Are' [video file], https://www.ted.com/talks/amy_cuddy_your_body_language_shapes_who_you_are?language=en (June 2012).

Page 105: McCraty, Rollin, *et al.* 'The Resonant Heart'. Institute of Heartmath [website], https://www.heartmath.org/assets/uploads/2015/01/the-resonant-heart.pdf (2005).

CHAPTER 4: CELEBRATE
Clance, Pauline R. and Suzanne A. Imes. 'The Imposter Phenomenon in High Achieving Women: Dynamics and Therapeutic Intervention.' *Psychotherapy Theory, Research and Practice* 15, no. 3 (1978): 241–247, doi:10.1037/h0086006.

Page 121: Sandberg, Sheryl. *Lean In: Work, and the Will to Lead* (Penguin Random House, 2015), p. ???

Page 135: Neff, Kristin. *Self Compassion: Stop Beating Yourself Up and Leave Insecurity Behind* (Yellow Kite Books 2011), p. 49.

Page 136: Whitworth, Laura, *et al., Co-Active Coaching: Changing Business Transforming Lives.* (Nicholas Brealey Publishing, 3rd edn., 2011).

CHAPTER 5: COMMIT
Alhola, Paula and Pälvi Polo-Kantola. 'Sleep Deprivation: Impact on Cognitive Performance.' *Neruopsychiatr Dis Treat* 3, no. 5 (2007): 553–567, PMID: 19300585.

Page 143: Gómez-Pinilla, Fernando. 'Brain Foods: The Effects of Nutrients on Brain Function.' Nat Rev Neurosci 9, no. 7 (2008): 568–578, doi:10.1038/nrn2421.

Pu, Hongjian, *et al.* 'Omega-3 Polyunsaturated Fatty Acid Supplementation Improves Neurologic Recovery and Attenuates White Matter Injury After Experimental Traumatic Brain Injury. *J Cereb Blood Flow Metab* 33, no. 9 (2013):1474-84, doi: 10.1038/jcbfm.2013.108.

Erickson, Kirk, *et al.* 'Physical Activity, Brain, and Cognition.' *Current Opinion in Behavioral Sciences* 4 (August 2015): 27–32, doi:10.1016/j.cobeha.2015.01.005.

BIBLIOGRAPHY

Arbinger Institute. *The Anatomy of Peace: How to Resolve the Heart of Conflict.* Penguin Books, 2006.

Barrett, Richard. *What My Soul Told Me.* Fulfilling Books, 2012.

Dispenza, Joe. *Evolve Your Brain: The Science of Changing Your Mind.* HCI Books, 2007.

Elrod, Hal. *The Miracle Morning: The 6 Habits That Will Transform Your Life Before 8AM.* John Murray Learning, 2016.

Glasser, William. *Choice Theory: A New Psychology of Personal Freedom.* HarperCollins, 1998.

Hay, Louise. *Heal Your Body: The Mental Causes for Physical Illness and the Metaphysical Way to Overcome Them.* Hay House, 1982.

Hay, Louise. *You Can Heal Your Life.* Hay House, 1984.

Hendricks, Gay. *The Big Leap: Conquer Your Hidden Fear and Take Life to the Next Level.* Harper One, 2009.

Huffington, Ariana. *Thrive.* WH Allen, 2014.

Ikonn, Alex, and Uj Ramdas. *The Five Minute Journal: The Simplest, Most Effective Thing You Can Do Every Day to be Happier.* Intelligent Change Inc., 2018.

Jeffers, Susan. *Feel the Fear and Do It Anyway.* Arrow Books, 1987.

Kavanaugh, Philip. *Magnificent Addiction: Discovering Addiction as Gateway to Healing.* Aslan Publishing, 1992.

Kline, Nancy. *Time to Think: Listening to Ignite the Human Mind.* Cassell, 2002.

Levine, Amir, and Rachel Heller. *Attached: Identify your Attachment Style and Find Your Perfect Match.* Rodale, 2011.

Neff, Kristin. *Self- Compassion: Stop Beating Yourself Up and Leave Insecurity Behind.* Yellow Kite Books, 2011.

Rankin, Lissa. *The Fear Cure: Cultivating Courage as Medicine for the Body, Mind and Soul.* Hay House, 2015.

Rubin, Gretchin. *Better than Before: What I learned About Making and Breaking Habits.* Two Roads, 2015.

Ruiz, Don Miguel. *The Four Agreements: A Practical Guide to Personal Freedom.* Amber-Allen Publishing, 1997.

Siegel, Daniel. *Mindsight: Transform Your Brain with the New Science of Kindness.* Oneworld Publications, 2010.

Sinek, Simon. *Start with Why.* Penguin Group, 2011.

Stanny, Barbara. *Overcoming Underearning: Overcome Your Money Fears and Earn What You Deserve.* Harper Business, 2005.

Tolle, Eckhart. *The Power of Now.* Hodder Mobius, 2005.

Walker, Matthew. *Why We Sleep: The New Science of Sleep and Dreams.* Scribner, 2017.

Ware, Bronnie. *The Top Five Regrets of the Dying: A life Transformed by the Dearly Departing.* Hay House, 2012.

Whitworth, Laura, Karen Kimsey-House, Henry Kimsey-House, and Philip Sandahl. *Co-Active Coaching: Changing Business Transforming Lives.* Nicholas Brealey Publishing, 2011.

Woodward Thomas, Katherine. *Calling in "The One": 7 weeks to Attract the Love of Your Life.* Harmony Books, 2004.

THANKS
An expression of gratitude

I have so many people I am grateful to and want to thank for helping me along the way: Victoria for 'getting' me and what *Change Your Life in 5* is about (and *finally* believing in the concept of sabotaging voices); Kathryn for helping me let go of *total* control and for taking care of business while I wrote this book; everyone at CTI involved in bringing the Co-Active model into the world – it literally changed my life; every single one of my amazing, courageous clients that I have worked with over the years – you have each shown me the courage and resilience of the human spirit through adversity; Dee for your holding, insights, and vast patience; Alison, my childhood best friend and the first person I ever coached – such a beautiful soul, I miss you; my soul sisters – as an only child you are my family of choice – thank you for seeing me through, holding me in the difficult times, as well as the joyous ones; Lou for the fun times during the dark days; Anne for your deep care and off-the-scale thoughtfulness; Elaine for backing me when I needed it the most; Lisa for your beautiful championing, hippy wisdom, and love; Nairy for your true championing and wonderful style darling; Sophie for your huge heart, beautiful energy and warmth; Veronique for your deep wisdom and for breaking me in; Nicola, for 30 years of love and friendship and making sure we stay connected when we're thousands of miles apart; Lisa S, for literally picking me up off the floor and being a brilliant woman; Kate, my fierce, loyal sister, you gave me much-needed tough love and daily support when I was spinning out writing this book. And much, much more. Mange-tout bird. Judy, what can I say? You believed in me from day one and made me feel safe, held and seen, like never before. You are a huge inspiration to the rest of us whipper-snapper coaches who have come up in the ranks behind you; Jason for being the loving, caring Dad that you are to Amelie; Milly for coming into our lives and loving Amelie the way you do, and for supporting me in the final days of writing this book; Mum and Dad, thank you for loving me and for supporting me in living this radically different lifestyle – I know it's given you grey hairs and many a sleepless night; Ben – well, I always hoped a man like you existed, and then here you are. Thank you for accepting me with all my foibles, for your early morning coffee, for your patience during the writing of this book, and for just being wonderful you; Amelie for opening my heart and showing me the depths of true, unconditional love. I love you all the way to the moon and back.

Picture credits

ShutterstockPhotoInc. 14–15 Noppanun K; 32, 49, 65, 95, 103, 116, 122, 137, 147 MJgraphics; 54–55 Alex Landa; 92–93 lukpedclub; 112–113 Semanche; 140–141 Sylverarts Vectors; 157 Anita Ponne

Eddison Books Limited

Managing Director Lisa Dyer
Senior Commissioning Editor Victoria Marshallsay
Copy Editor Katie Hewett
Designer Transmission
Proofreader Anna Cheifetz
Indexer Christine Shuttleworth
Production Gary Hayes